THE LOVE OF
SAILING

THE LOVE OF
SAILING
Douglas Phillips-Birt

OCTOPUS

First published 1976 by Octopus Books Limited,
59 Grosvenor Street, London W.1

© 1976 Octopus Books Limited
ISBN 0 7064 0453

Produced by Mandarin Publishers Limited
22a Westlands Road, Quarry Bay, Hong Kong

Printed in Hong Kong

Contents

Early Sailing Boats

It will never be known when men first set a sail. All that may be given is an approximate date for the earliest evidence of sail. At present this is provided by a small clay model found in southern Mesopotamia which shows what may have been a mast step and also the means of fixing shrouds. The date of the model is about 3,500 B.C. An indisputable sailing ship is painted on a vase dated 3,200–2,900 B.C. found in southern Egypt. How long before these vague dates the sail was used

cannot be known; it may have been several thousand years.

The square sail and its associated rigging was developed in the east and the Mediterranean in competition, as a means of propulsion, with the paddle and pivoted oar. Ships grew in size, sails in area and rigging in complexity, the problem being to give adequate strength to rigs composed of fragile sail fabrics and ropes. Square-sailed craft spread over the Aegean and the open Mediterranean between Egypt and Crete, the Red Sea and the Persian Gulf. The records that have survived of the early sea-going sailors are very sparse; Cretians, Egyptians, Greeks rowed and sailed over the summer seas of these areas, but even the Phoenicians, who rounded Africa and may have reached Britain, left little record of their sailing techniques. When the Mediterranean had become a Roman lake it was dominated in war by the galleys, which carried a square sail for auxiliary propulsion, and in trade by the biggest ships yet built, the grain ships propelled by a single large square sail on the main mast and a second small sail forward to give some assistance to the vessels' lumbering manoeuvrability. By this time men may have been using sail for 6,000 years.

When Julius Caesar reached Gaul and Britain he found sail being used in this dim north-western area where civilization petered out. But curiously enough yet further north, where the

Vikings' great tradition of seamanship was incubating, the kind of hull and steering arrangements capable of making use of sail were not evolved until about 700 A.D. Meanwhile the use of sail in the more southern coasts of Europe facing the Atlantic appears to have declined. Neither the Anglo-Saxons nor the later peoples of the Migration period seem to have used sail in their crossings to the offshore island of Britain.

While the Viking galleys with their single square sail reached a degree of performance still to be admired, in the Mediterranean a revolution had occurred in the means of sail setting and handling. After the death of their prophet Mohammed the Arabs swept from their burning deserts and in establishing an empire became the new masters of Mediterranean seafaring. And the rig they used, spreading it before them over the whole inland sea, was not the square rig which had served man for so long in his ocean voyaging, but the lateen, a form of fore-and-aft rig.

All sails may be divided broadly into two generic classes. We have considered above only the first devised of these and the simplest in concept, the square sail hung from a yard at its head and with the yard slung before the mast at the mid-point of the former. When driving the ship the wind always blows on the same side of the sail. The fore-and-aft sail in contrast is hinged on the mast in the fashion of a gate, and being free to swing from side to side the wind plays first on one surface of the sail and then on the other, depending on the wind's direction and how the sail is trimmed. A more subtle propulsive power is thus derived. While, along the coasts of northern Europe, the square sail remained dominant, for 500 years the Mediterranean was the sea of the lateen until, in the Medieval period, features of the northern and Mediterranean rig were merged to produce the three-masted ship which has been described as the 'master tool of western civilization'.

It was this rig, a mechanically complex combination of square and fore-and-aft sails, which opened up the oceans of the world during the ages of discovery and, until steam power replaced sail, propelled the most important types of ocean-going ships, naval and commercial. Such ships are today represented only by the few largest sail-training vessels. The smaller craft of the Mediterranean continued using the lateen rig. Meanwhile the fore-and-aft rig spread to other more northern shores in varying forms. If the three-masted square-rigged ship was the tool of the ocean seamen, the fore-and-aft rig became that of the coastal seamen, of fishermen and short passage traders. The lug and cutter rigs, and later the schooner as developed in America, were particularly suitable for the more confined waters where the ability to sail close to the wind was a prime requirement, and where the dangers of the lee shore close at hand and of shoals in estuary waters made good powers of manoeuvrability so important.

The transition from sail to steam power was the most tremendous revolution ever to affect ships. It occurred swiftly in relation to the long history of marine craft, though considered from the human point of view it occupied more than the average lifetime even in the most technically advanced areas of the world. The change was occurring at the time when yachting was first becoming a fashionable activity. The smaller craft of the last sailing navies, the cutters, despatch boats and so on, were fore-and-aft rigged to give them greater handiness, and it was these craft which served as the models for the early yachts, together with the fast craft of the revenue services and pilots. The schooner *America*, which in 1851 won the cup which has since become famous under her name, was basically a Sandy

Hook pilot boat. It was believed that the care and expense devoted to yachts would enable them to improve the breed of smaller working craft, particularly those of the navies.

Increasingly sail was replaced by mechanical power while the yacht was developed independently for its specialized purposes of racing and relaxation. The former has evolved, in terms purely of speed, into the most efficient craft in the long history of sail. And still today in the less developed parts of the world sail is working in the service of man, on the coasts of India and east Pakistan, in many other Asian and Chinese waters, and in corners of the Mediterranean where sail perhaps first ventured out of the rivers on to the broader back of that not always blue sea.

PAGES 6–7: A variety of Dutch seventeenth century vessels appear in this picture. The central ship showing her stern displays a typically Dutch feature of decoration at this time, a large painting spread over her stern like a mural picture, which the Dutch – in contrast to the French, whose ships were then over-loaded with a mass of gilded carving – often used as the central decorative feature. The scene shown in the picture might have some connection with the ship's name. The flat, or transom, stern usual in Dutch ships is also evident here. The large ship to the left is

a two-decker (i.e. has two decks of guns). Men may be seen out on the main topsail yard furling the canvas; beneath them the mainsail is already furled on its yard. A pinnace in the foreground is being pulled out to this ship.

OPPOSITE LEFT: The Brixham trawlers were amongst the most famous British fishing vessels in the days of sail, until their depletion during the inter-war years as the West Country harbour became emptied of trawlers and later filled with yachts. The trawlers were favoured by some deep water cruising yachtsmen who required capable sea-going craft at not too great an expense, and a number were converted into yachts. The rig typifies the working boats' kind of gaff ketch at its most efficient; it was commonly described as the 'Dandy rig'.

ABOVE: The cutter yacht *Blue Bell*, of the mid-nineteenth century, is shown engaging in several interesting operations of old-time cutter seamanship. Her topmast is on end (i.e. raised but the topsail has not yet been hoisted). It will be seen that the mainsail area has been temporarily reduced by lifting the lower fore part of the sail off the boom, an operation known as 'scandalizing'. The tack of the sail (i.e. the lower corner at the mast) is triced up and a quick sail reduction thereby affected. The jib is set on the long bowsprit, and the staysail abaft it is just in the process of being hoisted. In the distance another cutter is to be seen with her square-shaped fore-and-aft topsail set.

LEFT: Sail was first set by man at some unknown date, possibly in the fourth millenium B.C. We can only date – and that no more than approximately – the first evidence available of sail. This may be a clay model, c. 3500 B.C., found in southern Mesopotamia, which shows evidence (not conclusive) that the prototype set a simple square sail. An indisputable sailing craft is shown in a picture on an Egyptian vase dated about 3000 B.C., possibly earlier. The model shown here is of an Egyptian sailing ship of about 2000 B.C., of advanced design compared with the first sail of which there is record, but the basic square sail of the model with a boom along its foot represents the rudimentary sail from which the others have developed.

CENTRE LEFT: Though magnificent seamen, for various reasons sail was set late amongst the Vikings, not until about 700 A.D. This model of the Viking longship is based on the remains of a Viking galley recovered in excellent preservation at Gokstad, Norway. It is a rudimentary square sail that is hoisted without a boom, unlike the Egyptian sail, but the rigging is such that it might be trimmed and set to give an adequate sailing performance. The date of the galley is 900 A.D. The single square sail with which it was propelled on long voyages remained essentially unchanged in northern Europe until the single-masted sailing ship was replaced for ocean going by the three-masted, in the course of the fifteenth century.

BELOW LEFT: The smaller and simpler types of craft using sail were often little changed during the course of centuries. The Norwegian herring boats, models of which are shown here, have carried the deep impress of the Viking galley across 1000 years. The larger craft set the Viking square sail similarly rigged above the same kind of double-ended hull with clinker (overlapping) planking. The swinging sheer of the gunwale, the gracious lines, repeat those of the ships which the Vikings pushed down the fjord beaches when they set off raiding and pillaging.

ABOVE: The three-masted ship which was developed in the course of the fifteenth century has been described as the 'master tool of western civilization'. It was the three-masted ship which opened the oceans of the world to western man and made possible the great voyages of discovery. Drake's *Golden Hind*, the first ship to sail round the world (1577–1581) was not a large example of the three-masted ship of her time; the illustration shows a replica of Drake's ship which is sailing today. Famous though the ship was, and in her own day considered worthy of preservation – when for 100 years she lay in a drydock at Deptford on the river Thames – no details were kept of the vessel, and her dimensions had to be reconstructed from those of the drydock. She was probably about 60ft (18·29m.) from stem to sternpost.

ABOVE: *Mayflower* is representative of the type of smaller three-masted ship of the early seventeenth century. The seven sails she normally carried were typical of the day; on the mizzen was set a lateen, a Mediterranean contribution to the northern three-master, which in later centuries was changed to a northern gaff sail. The behaviour of the *Mayflower* replica, illustrated here, when she crossed the Atlantic provided interesting evidence about the sailing qualities of such a ship. Her average speed on the Atlantic passage was only four and a half knots, but in a good fair wind she maintained a seven knots average for 24 hours. She proved closer winded than expected, and showed remarkable ghosting ability in light airs.

LEFT: From time immemorial the sail of the China seas has been the balanced lug, with the sail having a yard at its head and a boom along the foot, both of which project ahead of the mast, so that about a fifth of the sail area lies before the mast. In the Chinese form of the rig the sail is crossed by many battens; a complex

system of sheets leads from these to control the sails. The rigging and character of sail are in marked contrast to the square sails of the Egyptian, Viking and modern Norwegian fishing boats. In recent years yachtsmen have caused a revival of interest in the Chinese lug by adapting its leading features but using modern, light materials, including aluminium alloy spars and terylene sails and rigging; and doing so not for antiquarian zeal but to produce an effective modern cruising rig.

RIGHT: This seventeenth century Dutch merchantman is running before heavy wind and seas with all sails furled but the foresail and mainsail. It is worth mentioning that at this time the term 'course' rather than 'sail' was beginning to be applied to the lowest square sail on each of the masts. Dutch ships of this type, of moderate size, were not strikingly different from English merchant ships of the same period. The rig, of six sails when all canvas was set, had not changed much since a century earlier. There is a whale in the foreground in danger of being run down.

LEFT: *Enigma* was an iron cutter of the same period as *Gazelle* (top right). She is shown here sailing without topsail and with her topmast housed. Several features of the rig of the time may be seen here: the very long bowsprit, which would be reefed, or run inboard, when a jib was not set, relieving the boat in heavy seas of considerable weight far forward, as the reefed topmast was able to reduce top weight; the loose-footed mainsail (i.e. the mainsail not laced to its boom) producing a baggy sail accentuated by the fact that· flax was the material of the sails. When the *America* came to England in 1851 she was able to disturb the yachtsmen of the then premier yachting nation by the superiority of her hard, flat, cotton sails, laced to the spars.

ABOVE: The clipper ship *Anglesey* is seen here with her royal yards bare above the topgallant sails. The topsails and topgallants are not divided into upper and lower sails as in later and larger square riggers. The term 'clipper', today often inexactly used and never very precisely defined, was applied to fast cargo ships in which carrying capacity was sacrificed to the fine lines demanded by speed; their service was mostly required for carrying valuable and quickly deteriorating cargoes, notably tea. In them the pursuit of speed sometimes became such an enthusiasm, even on the part of hard-headed ship-owners, that it outstripped too nice a regard for operating costs.

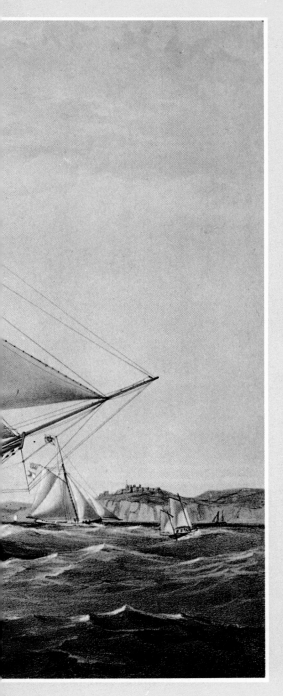

TOP RIGHT: The Royal Thames Yacht Club, which celebrated its bicentenary in 1975, is the second oldest yacht club in the British Isles, its senior being the Royal Cork Yacht Club whose records date back to 1720. Here the cutter *Gazelle* is in the process of crossing the finishing line as winner of the Royal Thames Yacht Club Grand Challenge Cup in 1840. She is a typical cutter of the day with a round bow and a great spread of canvas surmounted by a large square-headed topsail. In 1840 yachting, in which Britain led the world, had not yet swung into the era of rich Victorian growth, yacht design had not yet become an independent art, and yachts such as *Gazelle* retained many of the characteristics of the smaller naval craft and those of the revenue service, amongst which were found the smartest sailing craft of an earlier day.

BELOW RIGHT: The schooner *America*, which won the cup later offered for international competition as the America's Cup, came to the Solent in 1851. She was disconcertingly different from British yachts, then considered the finest in the world. 'The glorified pilot boat' was one English description of her, correct to the extent that in both hull and rig she was directly derived from the Sandy Hook pilot craft. Her low and rakish hull was of a shape unfamiliar in Britain, and her schooner rig, set on two extremely raking masts, had rigging of the utmost simplicity and flat cotton sails, which were an example to the Solent yachts in that summer of 1851. Later, under British ownership, the simplicity and ruggedness of the rig shown in the illustration, was changed to that of the more typically British schooner, carrying more sails, more rigging, but hardly attaining very much more efficiency.

Tall Ships
and Sail Training

It was a new and brilliant sight for the world of the 1950s when what became known as the Tall Ships gathered in Torbay, England, for the start of a race to Lisbon. It was 1956 and the first event of the Sail Training Association, which in the years since then has been organizing races for various types and sizes of craft. These range from the largest square-rigged vessels still afloat today, the ships, barques, brigantines and brigs of the nations which practise sail training on a large scale, to top-sail and staysail schooners and relatively small yachts rigged as ketches and sloops.

The Sail Training Association, a company 'limited by guarantee and not for profit' whose Patron is the Duke of Edinburgh, has an international Advisory Committee drawn from seventeen nations. It operates for the benefit of two kinds of young people. On the one hand are those who are being trained as future officers or ratings in the naval or mercantile services. That sail training still has a value, commensurate with the great expense involved, for the education of professional seamen in the 1970s is not a view accepted by all, but it is widely enough held by those with considerable sea-going experience in the modern world to be generally supported. On the other hand are those for whom sail training is part of a general education. For them voyages in sailing craft provide briefly a fresh and exciting way of life that can hardly do other than benefit all normal young people and possibly raise new interests through the broadening effects of sea, travel and communal effort.

Captain Ernst von Witsendorf, for some years Master of the West German Navy training ship *Gorch Fock*, a three-masted barque of 1,727 tons Thames Measurement built as recently as 1958, has written thus:

'I do not see the big sailing ship, going on her way under sail, as being old fashioned or out of date, because I understand the large square-rigged ship as a unique school for character building, as a trust to hand on for the benefit of young people so that they can meet each other in the spirit of real adventure which is so rare in this materialistic world.'

Assuredly in such ships as the above – in the Danish three-masted full-rigged ship *Danmark*, the Russian four-masted barque *Kruzenshtern*, the Polish full-rigged ship *Dar Pomorza*, the Argentinian three-masted ship *Libertad*, the Italian *Amerigo Vespucci*, the British three-masted topsail schooners *Sir Winston Churchill* and *Malcolm Miller* or the brig *Royalist* – people are able to look upon a kind of sea beauty that would have disappeared for ever but for the Sail Training Association. It is impressive to observe the enthusiasm with which the crowds pack the sea shore and the numerous spectator craft that gather round when these tall ships appear.

It is laid down in the Association's 'Racing and Sailing Rules' that not less than 50 per cent of the working complement of competing vessels must consist of persons under training in the above categories. A lower age limit of sixteen years, with fifteen years for Class A, is set for trainees – Class A comprising the largest training ships. For the major Sail Training races, which are normally those in which Class A is eligible to compete, the upper age limit is 25 years. It is generally intended that trainees should not include those who already spend much of their time sailing regularly in the offshore races of the yachting fleets, such as those organized by the Royal Ocean Racing Club, and including such internationally famous races as the Fastnet, the Sydney-Hobart, the Rhode Island-Bermuda, which are considered in another chapter.

There are two broad divisions in the classes of vessel sailed in the Sail Training Association's events. The big class includes

such vessels as those mentioned above; they must exceed 150 tons Thames Measurement and there is no upper limit of size. A vessel such as the *Gorch Fock* carries twelve officers and a permanent crew of 59 seamen; the full complement of trainees is 100. The smaller British *Malcolm Miller*, of 299 tons Thames Measurement compared with 1,727 tons, carries 8 officers, 3 permanent crew and 44 trainees.

Class B includes all other sailing vessels with normally a low limit of 30ft (9·14m.) length on the waterline. This limit may be dropped to 24ft (7·32m.) waterline in certain races – as, for example, the cruise in company from the Solent to St. Malo which closed the 1974 programme of events.

It will be evident that a wide range of ship sizes are involved in Sail Training events, as small as 10 tons and up to more than 3,000 tons; also a wide range of rigs from the nimble sloop evolved in the yachting fleets to the full-rigged ships and barques descended from ocean-trading ships of an earlier generation. The former type of craft can work to windward with great

efficiency; the square-riggers need a free wind and a respectable amount of it to keep going. The vessels are sub-divided into classes for racing, narrowing the disparity of size, while a handicapping or time allowance system further compensates for differences in rig and speed potential.

The character of the sailing programme for a season may be judged by that of 1974. There were two sets of races, in the English Channel/Bay of Biscay area and in the Baltic, for which the fleets assembled in July at Dartmouth and Copenhagen for races to Corunna and Gdynia respectively, distances of 470 and 247 nautical miles. The Corunna fleet remained in Spain until the 26th July, while crews were interchanged and made a cruise in company. There followed a return race of 560 miles from Corunna to the Nab Tower (east of Portsmouth). Meanwhile the Gdynia fleet also sailed for the Solent, where many thousand people were able to watch an inspiring display of sail at the beginning of August as the combined fleets sailed past Southsea Castle.

PAGES 16–17: The Tall Ships races have been described as a vehicle of the modern world's nostalgia. The public interest aroused when the fleet gathers at any port is an indication of how widespread and potent that nostalgia is. Since the races started, the ports that have seen the fleets make a roll call of the European waterfront: Cherbourg, Gothenburg, Torbay, Lisbon, Naples, Oslo, Ostend, Portsmouth, Plymouth, Falmouth, Weymouth, Helsinki, Gdynia, Corunna, Tenerife, Malta, Rotterdam, Copenhagen. In 1964 the three classes of the fleet, numbering 12 vessels, visited Bermuda.

ABOVE: A god's eye view but not yet at the masthead. . . .
It is a feature of the square rig, as opposed to the fore-and-aft rig, that its handling requires constant work aloft, and this is one of the features of sail training considered to be particularly valuable. The two British Sail Training Association ships, basically fore-and-aft rigged, have square elements in their rig of the fore topsails; likewise schooners such as *Belle Poule* and *L'Etoile*.

LEFT: The British Sail Training Association ships in company, *Malcolm Miller* with *Sir Winston Churchill* down to leeward.

ABOVE: The Sail Training ship *Sir Winston Churchill* was designed specially for the purpose by the yacht architects Laurent Giles and Partners of Lymington, Hampshire, and built by Richard Dunston Ltd, Yorkshire, for the British Sail Training Association, who have been responsible financially for maintaining the ship in commission and organizing her schedules. She was launched in 1966. The ship carries a modern version of the three-masted topsail schooner rig, and is here seen under full sail. The foremast carries the square topsail, the mizzen is a Bermudian (or triangular) sail; the gaff foresail and mainsail carry topsails; ahead is a staysail, inner and outer jibs and jib topsail. Staysails are also carried between the masts. With all set here but the square topsails *Sir Winston Churchill* presents a proud display of canvas.

OPPOSITE ABOVE: *Malcolm Miller*, a sister ship to *Sir Winston Churchill*, was launched just twenty months later. Here she is seen under reduced canvas. Out on the bowsprit members of the crew are preparing to hoist the jib topsail. The fore and main topsails and the square topsails are not yet set. The rigs of these two ships offer an idea of the kind of sail that might be working round the coast of the United Kingdom and over to the continent today had mechanical power not displaced sail for commercial purposes.

OPPOSITE BELOW: *Creole* was built as a yacht in 1927 by the famous English firm of yacht builders Camper and Nicholsons, and this magnificent 700 tons staysail schooner was one of her designer's favourite creations. Her early years were unhappy thanks to unknowledgeable owners, one of whom drastically reduced the rig by cutting down the masts. She was later restored and became one of the most admired of yachts. Here she is seen running before the wind, an unfavourable point of sailing for such a rig, but making a handsome best of it with a large balloon spinnaker at the foremast and with her mizzen staysail boomed out to starboard. *Creole* was a prominent participant in the early sail-training races.

ABOVE: Whenever she appears amongst the Tall Ships the huge Italian *Amerigo Vespucci* is liable to capture most attention. A towering two-decker, her style of painting recalls an earlier day than her own, though she herself is not young, having been built in Castellmare 44 years ago, though extensively refitted in 1964. She carries a complement of 550. The funnel, rising amongst the masts and yards of her ship rig, is able to recall the days when engines were first installed in large sailing ships and the well known evolution was performed 'up funnel and down screw' as the mechanical propulsion was brought into operation. *Amerigo Vespucci* has diesel-electric motors developing 1,900 horse-power (1400 kW) which are able to drive the heavy ship at 10½ knots.

RIGHT: The French *Belle Poule* belongs to the Ecole Navale and with a Thames Measurement tonnage of 225 tons she is slightly smaller than *Sir Winston Churchill* and *Malcolm Miller*. She carries a permanent crew of eleven and twenty trainees compared with the eleven crew and 44 trainees of the latter ships. A two-masted topsail schooner, she is seen here with all sail set except for the upper square topsail. The wind is not strong and she carries a light balloon forestaysail and a large main staysail between the masts above the gaff foresail. *Belle Poule* was built in 1932. The name of this elegant ship is more tactfully translated as *Beautiful Bird* than *Beautiful Hen*. France also runs *L'Etoile*, a similar topsail schooner.

FAR RIGHT: *Danmark*, like *Dar Pomorza*, is a three-masted ship. These two vessels present to us today the rig that was common in the fastest clippers about 100 years ago, when their names were household words and homes all over the country awaited with interest the arrival of the clippers from China with their cargoes of the season's first tea. Such famous ships as the *Taeping*, *Ariel*, *Flying Cloud*, *Thermopylae* amongst the most celebrated of them, and *Cutty Sark*, now in drydock at Greenwich, England, were all three-masted

ships and the fastest sailing vessels afloat. Other three-masted ships in the Sail Training fleet are the *Georg Stage* and *Sorlandet*.

OPPOSITE: The Polish *Dar Pomorza* is a heavyweight in the grandest manner, with a Thames Measurement tonnage of 1,784 tons. She is able to carry no less than 100 trainees, a permanent crew of 30 hands and ten officers. *Dar Pomorza* is a ship, as opposed to a barque, being square-rigged on all three masts. This view from ahead gives a striking impression of the array of headsails carried, named, from the lowest, fore topmast staysail, inner jib, outer jib, flying jib, fore royal jib. She carries the traditional type of stocked anchors catted on either side of the fo'c'sle.

LEFT: *Centurion* carries the rig, unusual among Sail Training ships, known as hermaphrodite brig, though this elaborate piece of nomenclature is usually simplified into the term brigantine; which is, however, sometimes regarded as a slightly different rig. The mainmast (aft) carries fore-and-aft sails, a mainsail and gaff topsail; the foremast carries square canvas and usually more sails than the two set by *Centurion*, whose rig is indeed unconventional in several respects. In the days when the hermaphrodite brig was a not uncommon rig, there were four or five square sails on the foremast, named foresail, fore lower topsail, fore upper topsail, fore topgallant sail, fore royal. These are the names of the sails on the foremasts of ships and barques, as for example on the foremast of the *Gorch Foch* and the *Dar Pomorza* (page 23). Sometimes in the largest ships, the topgallant sails are split like the topsails into an upper and lower sail. The mast then sets six square sails. The splitting of topsails and topgallant sails into upper and lower parts was a late development in the square rig not usually practised in the days of the fastest clippers. It was suitable for the last and largest commercial sailing ships.

BELOW LEFT: Compared with the great barques and ships at the heavyweight end of the Sail Training fleet the Sea Cadet Corps' brig *Royalist*, of 110 tons Thames Measurement, is of modest size. She carries 26 trainees and a permanent crew of six. A brig is a two-masted vessel, square-rigged on both masts; but like three- and four-masted ships she carries also on the mast at the stern a fore-and-aft gaff sail, the spanker, which may be clearly seen in the picture of *Royalist*. Her hull shows the traditional decorative style of painted gunports which was common amongst the last ocean-going commercial sailing ships. The crew are in the process of hoisting the fore staysail.

RIGHT: With *Gorch Fock* we are amongst the heavyweights again, a fine modern three-masted barque of 1,727 Thames Measurement tons, built for the Federal Republic of Germany in 1958. She carries 120 trainees and a permanent crew of 72 including thirteen officers. The three fore-and-aft sails on the mizzen mast are named respectively, from the bottom, lower spanker, upper spanker and gaff topsail. The *Gorch Fock* has been a consistent performer in Sail Training Association events and is one of the smartest vessels in the international fleets which assemble for them.

Class Racing round the Buoys

The classical mode of yacht racing is over relatively short regatta courses during the daylight hours. It used to be believed there could be no sport and an appreciable lack of seamanship in racing in the dark. Only during recent decades has a high proportion of the racing between yachts of any size been conducted over longer courses with distances entailing day and night sailing – not necessarily ocean racing, but more precisely offshore racing. But the yachts that engage in this may also spend part of the time regatta racing. The combination of round the buoys and offshore racing which has been devised in recent years in such events as the Admiral's Cup and One Ton Cup is considered in the chapter on ocean racing.

Prior to 1939, when ocean racing was still something of a peripheral activity, the acme of yacht racing was considered to lie in the principle classes of the International Yacht Racing Union: the handful of great J-Class cutters, the long established 12-Metres, now mainly confined to America's Cup racing, the popular 8-Metre class, the numerous 6-Metres, the last being boats as big as many ocean racers today, but without a cabin and still remembered by some as the most perfect racing machines ever produced for the sport of short-distance yacht racing. None of these now race regularly as classes, though a few scattered and small 6-Metre fleets exist.

The 6-Metres were replaced by the 5·5-Metre class to another rule, producing a shorter, lighter, more economical class of boat. The new class gained a following in Scandinavia and is sailed in Bermuda and some European countries. In the United Kingdom it has never become popular but it gained on appearance the status of an Olympic class – the biggest of them.

The principle of the most highly developed round the buoys racing is that the boats are built to the same rating under the chosen rule, level racing then being possible with the eccentricities of time allowance eliminated; but the boats are not of one design and development in hull form and rig is possible within the limits of the measurement rule. Thus it is still in the 12-Metre America's Cup class, and was in the defunct 8- and 6-Metre classes; it remains so in the 5·5-Metre class. Increasingly round the buoys racing has been monopolized by small one-design classes, open dayboats of well known international classes or local classes indigenous to particular areas. A return

to level racing under free design conditions has been made however in the 'Ton' classes considered on page 56.

The Stars are the most remarkable type of one-design known to yachting, the most numerous and longest-lived kind of small racing keel boat in the yachting story. The first Stars were appearing on Long Island Sound as early as 1910. Half a century later there were more than 3,500 Stars scattered round the coasts of the world in more than 200 fleets. It was the first successful application of the one-design principle on a worldwide scale. It was intended to be the smallest and simplest possible keel boat fit for adult racing, and though ideas have now changed as to what sailing adults are capable of sustaining, the Stars shine on, continuing to hold their loyal thousands of supporters.

The Stars began as, and have remained, a class of open racing boat. The Dragon class began in 1929 in Sweden as a small, cheap cruiser-racer with an exciting performance and some rugged accommodation for young people consisting of two berths beneath a cabin top; it has since become a sophisticated and far from inexpensive international racing class, their cabin no more than a sail locker, and those who race them some of the finest, and not necessarily young, helmsmen in the world. Thus has occurred the metamorphosis of a knockabout, raised to Olympic racing status. A one-design class it remains, though under pressure of racing competition, built with the utmost refinement to the limits of the tolerances allowed. The rig was modernized in 1946.

Today, with the apparently secure dominating position in the yacht building industry gained by glass reinforced plastics and the moulding of hulls in series under factory conditions, it is hard to see that other than one-design classes can regain a place among the racing fleets of smaller boats. The creative side of small boat racing is deprived of its greatest charm.

PAGES 26–27: Offshore Class 2 is seen here mixed up with the X class. The latter are half-decked keel boats 20ft 8in. (6·3m.) in length with the shallow draught of 2ft 9in. (0·84m.). They typify the best kind of one-design class of an earlier day designed for local conditions – the Xs originally sailed in the Solent and Poole and Chichester harbours though they have spread further – but they are still the most popular Solent one-design class of keel boat and appear in numbers that impress each Cowes Week. Classes such as these, built of timber by traditional methods, face the question of survival today, the cost of new construction being excessive.

OPPOSITE FAR LEFT: Once known as the International Yacht Racing Union 6-Metre class, the Sixes were the smallest of the classes to the I.Y.R.U. rule, and also perhaps the most highly developed; superb\racing machines, some 24ft (7·32m.) in length on the waterline and 37ft (11·28m.) overall. They were without accommodation but very expensive, beautifully but lightly constructed, narrow, deep, and with some three-quarters of their total weight concentrated in the lead keel. Their costliness led to their being abandoned by the I.Y.R.U. after the Second World War, but their performance and beauty were able to compel the continuing loyalty of a few and they are still sometimes raced. One of them is the Australian *Pacemaker*, seen here, which has contested a series of matches against American 6-Metres.

OPPOSITE LEFT: To replace the 6-Metres the I.Y.R.U. introduced a new class to a different rule, which came into force at the beginning of 1950. These were the 5½-Metres, seen here racing under spinnakers in a reaching wind. They are smaller, very much lighter boats than the 6-Metres, averaging about 35ft (10·67m.) overall and 22ft (6·71m.) on the waterline, and being lighter have less proportionate weight in the ballast keel. In Britain the class has never had a big following, and nowhere has it gained the prestige of the 6-Metres, though it was early adopted as an Olympic class.

ABOVE: In the 90s of the last century there were boats in the Solent and on the Clyde known as Half-Raters. They did much to establish the amateur sport of racing in small but finely designed and built craft. Soon after the Second World War Uffa Fox designed the Flying Fifteen, measuring 15ft (4·57m.) overall, with a very light skimming dish form of hull and having a bulbed ballast keel, closely resembling some of the Half-Raters. The boats are one-design but the rules allow generous tolerances in dimensions and various methods of construction. Three Flying Fifteens are shown here racing in the Solent. Despite carrying a ballast keel, the boats plane readily and offer some of the liveliness of a dinghy combined with the smoother action of bigger keel boats.

LEFT: Today the gaff rig has almost totally disappeared from the inshore racing fleets, but it is still found in the racing classes of Dublin bay. One example is illustrated here, sailing off Dun Laoghaire. With a bowsprit and setting a jib and staysail, and a topsail with jackyard (the spar along the after edge of the topsail), such a yacht would have been a common enough sight early in the present century; today she refreshes the eye grown perhaps a little tired of the modern racing rigs, all too much like stark isosceles triangles.

BELOW: The One Ton cup was originally sailed for by yachts rating one ton under a measurement rule in force at the end of the last century. It passed subsequently to the 6-Metres (see page 28) which sailed for it regularly during a number of years. It was a celebrated old trophy when the *Cercle de la Voile de Paris*, holders of the cup, offered it in 1965 for yachts rating at 22ft (6·71m.) under the Royal Ocean Racing Club's rule. Thus the rule, and today the International Offshore Rule which has replaced that of the RORC, has been adopted for fixed rating inshore racing, round the buoys, as well as offshore and ocean racing. The illustrations show a

One Ton cup fleet crowded together soon after a windward start, below left, and a scene on board one of the yachts, below.

RIGHT: The Bembridge Redwings are one of the most interesting local classes on the coast of the United Kingdom. Sailed only by the Bembridge Sailing Club, for whom they were designed by Camper and Nicholsons, there have never been more than a few handfuls of them. The rules of the class have, however, enabled valuable experiments to be made in rig and sail plan, which have now been in progress since the later years of the last century. The original Redwing class was replaced by a new class, illustrated here, in 1937. Like the former Redwings, the present class has a one-design hull, but the sail plan may be of any kind whatever within the limit of not exceeding 200 square feet (18·58 sq.m.) in area. As a result, down the years the class has produced valuable if sometimes outlandish experiments in rig, particularly valuable during the period when the Bermudian sail plan was first being adopted for racing. The sail plans of Redwings have now become more closely alike though with small, if significant, differences.

LEFT: The famous Stars were the first one-design class to gain a large international following. The first of them came out in 1911, and were regarded at the time as the smallest boats suitable for racing by adults. Ideas since then have altered. Half a century later there were more than 3,500 Stars split into more than 200 fleets scattered round the coasts of the world, and during the early years of growth the Stars so far outnumbered any other racing class as to appear to belong to a different universe. The hull form is of the simplest possible, a chine hull with a nearly flat bottom, 22ft 7in. (6·88m.) in length with an iron bulbed fin and the rudder hung on a skeg. The hull remains as originally designed in 1911 but the rig has been changed twice since then. Stars carry a big area of canvas in comparison with average sail areas today, and they are indeed old fashioned in this respect, though advanced in the use of bending masts and other refinements of sail setting. The Stars were one of the Olympic classes until 1968. They are now being built in glass reinforced plastics.

ABOVE: The 5½-Metres, like the 6-Metres (see page 28), are built to a rule allowing flexibility and development in design. This inevitably adds to expense, but only thus can the creative side of yachting, the science and art of design, be fostered. Since the war the principle of one-design has, in the cause of economy, become dominant in racing inshore – round the buoys – and the classes used for the purpose, with the exception of the America's Cup 12-Metres (to the same measurement rule as the largely abandoned 6-Metres) are composed of small craft without accommodation. Of these one of the most popular is shown here, the International Dragon, boats of 29·2ft (9m.) overall, 18·17ft (5·54m.) on the waterline.

OPPOSITE ABOVE: The Dragons are an elderly class, designed in 1929 as a very small fast cruiser with minimal accommodation. Once adopted as an international racing class its development became notably at variance with the original intention of the design. Whilst retaining their one-design hull, the rigging details became those of the most sophisticated kind of inshore racing boat, and there was no longer any question of a boat in racing trim being used for cruising; the small cabin became a sail locker. It is not to be questioned today that the basic

hull of the Dragon, the design of which is approaching half a century in age, could be improved. Conceptions of a similar but more modern design are brought forward from time to time, and one such which has materialized into a class is known as the International One Design, as illustrated here, which is not strictly international as it happens. Slightly larger than the Dragon and with some accommodation, the yachts were introduced at Burnham, England, and race also in the Solent.

RIGHT: In 1965 the International Yacht Racing Union organized trials to select a new international two-man keel boat class. The Tempest proved outstandingly successful in the trials, winning eight out of nine selection races and having to retire from one with a broken rudder. The Tempest was given international status at the end of the year. They are very light keel boats 22ft (6·71m.) in length and weighing less than half a ton, with about 60 per cent of this weight in the steel fin and lead bulb. They have generous sail area and plane only a little less readily than an unballasted dinghy. Construction is in reinforced plastics and a number of builders throughout the world are licensed to build them.

Dinghies

In 1939 racing dinghies, though the numbers of them seemed at the time remarkable, formed only a tiny part of the sailing fleet. At the head of the dinghy list was the International 14ft class, which had brought prestige and a certain *chic* to dinghy racing; the Prince of Wales cup for this class was the most respected of trophies. The Fourteens were perhaps the most exquisite creations ever to be produced by boatbuilders in timber, and the class today, tiny in size compared with the massive fleets of other classes, retains its exclusive reputation.

But the seeds of the future lay, in 1939, in the 12ft National class, then only three years old. It represented a quite revolutionary conception on the part of the then Yacht Racing Association (today's Royal Yachting Association) – the smallest practicable two-man racing dinghy to be built as cheaply as possible. Though the rules were framed to emphasize cheapness, the Twelves, like the Fourteens, are not of one-design. There remained strong in 1939 the prejudice, now totally disappeared, which associated one-design with motor cars. Even a 12ft (3·66m.) dinghy intended to be as cheap as possible should be an individual creation of unique character.

Despite this the 12ft Nationals did anticipate the future by becoming in a considerable degree one-design; for when the journal 'Yachting World' sponsored the Uffa-King design by Uffa Fox it became so popular that boats built to these plans formed a considerable proportion of the class. Meanwhile at numerous places round the coast there were local dinghy

classes, numbered in handfuls, usually built by local boatbuilders; they were parochial and proud to be so. Open dinghy meetings were rare.

The Yacht Racing Association moved swiftly into the dinghy field on the return of peace, with the stated object of making small boat racing more easily available to youth. The Association introduced two new classes of one-design dinghy the smaller of which, the 12ft (3·66m.) Firefly, being adopted as an Olympic class, became quickly established. The immediate future of the racing dinghy was anticipated in this still active class; not only was it one-design, it was produced by factory methods, being hot moulded of timber veneers under pressure, or as more conservative people described it, cooked like a waffle instead of being built like a boat. It was a matter of only a few years before the proved effectiveness of moulding hull shells in glass reinforced plastics made possible the production of one-design classes some of which numbered thousands in a total dinghy fleet numbering millions. Such was the overwhelming success of the Yacht Racing Association's idea of 'making small boat racing more easily available to youth'; though the outcome was due largely to the efforts of independent designers, builders and sponsors. Sponsoring was an important element in the explosive growth of dinghy racing made possible in the Wellsian world where dinghies appeared by chemist out of factory.

The performance of dinghies was altered in an important respect. The capsizing of a dinghy had formerly been a small disaster, putting a boat firmly out of a race. Now by means of cunningly shaped decking and the provision of a big volume of intact buoyancy, dinghies were designed that might be righted after capsizing without outside help. A dinghy might race round a course capsizing at intervals and still come home the winner.

A world in which inflation and the cost of skilled labour were teaching everyone to 'do-it-himself', was obviously one in which 'build-it-yourself' dinghies would flourish. Initially this encouraged many classes of vee-bottom boats which might be constructed in salt water-resisting plywood and provided by the manufacturer in the form of a kit of parts. Surprisingly, this was a reversion to an old maritime practice. A century before anything like the modern racing dinghy had appeared the Shetlanders had been building their Scandinavian types of boat from sets of planks and parts sent from Norway. It has been suggested that the oldest surviving vessel in the world, the ship of Cheops, found buried near the Great Pyramid, was a very large building kit, the ship having been found in many hundreds of parts.

With dinghies becoming numbered in millions, and with the one-design principle enforced by the techniques of construction, the creation of a multitude of different classes was the only alternative to a most deadening national and international uniformity. The numerous classes of dinghy that appeared during the 1950s and 1960s and continue to appear, though the pace seems to be slackening, is not out of proportion to the total number of dinghies now in existence.

PAGES 34–35: The Fireball is almost as hot stuff as the name implies. It is a pure racing craft for inland and sheltered coastal waters, 16ft 2in. (4·93m.) in length, with a hull drawing 6½in. (16·5cm.) with the centreboard up, 4ft 9in. (1·45m.) with it lowered, and weighing 175lb. (79·38kg.). The beam is not excessive at 4ft 8½in. (1·44m.); on the other hand the sail area is generous; the trapeze, shown in action in the photograph, is necessary for all but a heavy crew in order to keep the boat upright when beating to windward in a moderate breeze.

The hull is particularly suitable for amateur construction from kits, and a high proportion – probably the majority – of the class is believed to have been produced thus. Originally hulls were of plywood; later glass plastics were permitted.

Introduced in 1962, the immediate and rapid growth of the class was enough to impress even minds bemused by the numbers in modern dinghy classes. The awful statistics were produced that one new boat was joining the class for each day of the year (including Sundays no doubt) and it is not surprising that the class soon soared to more than 2000 in numbers spread over a few score countries.

OPPOSITE LEFT: The Enterprise class is amongst the largest in the world, which is appropriate since it was conceived as 'the boat for the people'. The hull, 13ft 3in. (4·04m.) in length and weighing just less than 200lb. (90·71kg.), is of the simple double chine form,

as may be seen in the illustration – a compromise between the vee-bottom type and the round bilge. Numerous fleets of the Enterprise are racing, but the type is also used as a cruising and knockabout boat; our picture shows one sailing off Bahrain in the Arabian Gulf.

BELOW: The A class raters, seen here racing on their home waters on the Thames, at Bourne End, are closely related to the Half-Raters (page 29) and links with an even earlier period of yachting. Their origin lies in a nineteenth century rule of measurement produced by the then Yacht Racing Association, today's Royal Yachting Association. Their hulls are of the extreme dish or scow form, with centreboards, and in comparison with the average dinghy are large. Since the mid-1920s the A class raters have carried the Bermudian rig. Boats built in the early years of the present century continue to race, but it cannot be expected that any new boats of the type will be built.

LEFT: The Merlin-Rocket class was originally two separate classes founded by independent enthusiasts. The Merlin, of very advanced design and tricky to sail, gained much publicity through being sponsored by the journal 'Yachting World'; it was merged with the more conventional Rocket and in 1950 the combined class, then totalling 330 boats, received national status. The Merlin-Rockets did much to advance a modern concept in dinghy design. Here one of the class is seen planing under ideal conditions, the wind slightly abaft the beam and the boat sustaining a degree of lift, and with it a considerable acceleration.

BELOW LEFT AND RIGHT: The International 14ft class, still today the one with the greatest prestige amongst dinghies, brings us back to the earliest days of organized dinghy racing. But we need revert to no further than the early 1920s when rules for a National 14ft class were produced; these in effect codified the prevalent ideas of the important features of a good racing dinghy, while leaving design free within these limits to progress. And this it did, to lead step by step to the modern dinghy.

In the process the Fourteens became more exquisitely built and much more expensive, double skin planking with oiled silk between the layers replacing the original carvel planking, and details of fittings and rig becoming the subject of devoted attention. The liberal character of the class rules gave a freedom of design which allowed, in the Fourteens and the newer National 12ft class, the planing type of hull to be developed. Today the planing, or skimming, ability of racing dinghies is so much an intrinsic part of their character that its absence can hardly be imagined. Uffa Fox, more than anybody, led the way in evolving the skimming dinghy.

The Fourteens became an international class in 1927, in the year when the first race for the Prince of Wales Cup was sailed, and continued to lead the way in the development of racing dinghies in a world in which such boats were not yet multitudinous. But the Fourteens continued to show their salty, even seaweedy origin, being the sophisticated heirs of the yacht's tender. They were, as the illustration on the right shows, deckless and carried a big area of sail. The illustration, below left, shows two of the class racing for the Prince of Wales Cup at Torquay in 1975.

OPPOSITE LEFT: The Mirror dinghy is about as simple and inexpensive a boat with effective sailing performance, in modern terms, as may be devised. The hull, 10ft 10in. (3·3m.) long and weighing 135lb. (61kg.), is of pram form – that is, the bow instead of being pointed in plan has a transom, narrower and lifted higher above the water than the stern transom. The rig is a gunter lug, allowing a short and simply stayed mast with a single shroud per side.

LEFT: The Hornet, like the smaller Enterprise class (illustrated on page 36), is one of today's immensely popular types of racing dinghy. In the Hornet, 16ft (4·88m.) in length compared with the 13ft 3in. (4·04m.) of the Enterprise but with 8in. (20cm.) less beam and only 24lb. (10·8kg.) more weight if built down to the limit, the racing characteristics are rather more emphasized. As usual in today's dinghies, the hull and rig are one-design; a measure of design freedom is allowed in the layout of the cockpit and the design and placing of the fittings.

BELOW LEFT: The International 5–0–5 dinghy is a dedicated racing machine for a crew of two. It is a tightly controlled one-design class of exceptionally high performance designed for the experienced and carrying a generous amount of sail. As one helmsman in the class has said, 'You have to fight, coax and cajole these boats . . . but what a performance they have for their size . . . capsizes are the rough and tumble of racing these boats'.

In this last respect we see the difference between the modern dinghy and those of an earlier generation, particularly the 14ft International. A capsize in the latter meant the end of the day's sport. In the 5–0–5 dinghy and others you may capsize your way round the course and complete it even though you will not win. This is now regarded as a perfectly respectable nautical procedure.

ABOVE: Tiresome, but not the end of the race.

TOP: This is a close finish indeed in a Block Island Race Week event, on the east coast of the U.S.A.

ABOVE: The Sydney Harbour 18-footers have been staggering the sailing world for a long time. They have all the appeal of any extreme manifestation, and these boats have for some years provided displays of the sail-carrying urge pushed to its limit. Few in numbers, with no international following whatever – though they are sailed in a small number of other harbours in Australia and New Zealand – they have none the less gained an international reputation.

The 18-footers are not a one-design class. The length is limited and the minimum beam and depth also, ballast is not allowed, and the boats must be open or half-decked. But any amount of sail area may be carried, and any number of crew. The two latter provisions are the crux of

the matter. Never have there been boats of the size that have carried so much sail held upright by so many people. As someone once wrote of them: 'In a sailing world given over progressively to more and more desiccated erudition, the 18-footer is out for a good old fashioned sail and the devil take the hindermost'.

Not only the amount of sail but the variety set upon occasions – a gaff-rigged ringtail set outside a Bermudian mizzen, for example – brings the old clipper ship tradition of sporting fancy sails, which may in fact not do all that much good, back to the modern scene where science prevails. The newest boats are, however, more lightly built and carry sail plans in which aerodynamic efficiency replaces the former not undiscerning, but none the less reckless, generosity of sail spread.

RIGHT: 12-footers skip across Sydney harbour during a championship race.

Cruising Yachts

Until recent times the small cruiser was a Cinderella among yachts. Primarily this was because the professional architect could find little reputation or money in designing them. The standard cruiser of the types so common today was still a relative newcomer to the yachting scene in the immediate post-war years of the '40s, and even these were liable to be indifferently designed and built.

The situation earlier had been that small – 4–8 tons Thames Measurement – cruising yachts were not often seriously designed by anyone, while those slightly larger, in the 10–15 tons range, came occasionally from the boards of reputable designers, but at a price for individual building usually far beyond the means of the young men and married couples who wanted them. During the last years when timber was still the only material for building small cruisers, a number of builders produced small lines of stock cruisers, some of them respectable sea-going craft with simple accommodation for two to four people.

The revolution occurred with the development of glass reinforced plastics as a constructional material. At the first London Boat Show in 1955 the few moulded plastic boats, all very small, had been regarded with curiosity, and some of them with not unjustified disdain. There followed a galloping disappearance of timber as a constructional material until, by the time of the 1971 International Boat Show in London, of 117 yachts and motor sailers ranging in price between the modest and the extremely expensive there was one single wooden-hulled model exhibited. The term 'model', taken over from the mass producing world of cars, had now become commonly applied to classes of small cruising yacht, and the size of classes grew amazingly as the demand for small cruisers increased. When boats had been built of wood a class 40 strong had been considered something of a triumph; such a number has become totally unremarkable with the flight of leisure to

the coastal waters of the world.

It was a trend in which the U.S.A. led the way. As an experienced American observer, Robert N. Bavier, has observed: 'In summer months for eastern yachtsmen, cruising in New England offers hundreds of miles of scenic waters with literally thousands of harbours to choose from. . . . In the Pacific northwest excellent cruising grounds again abound, and naturally it is in this area that yachting is growing at as rapid a rate as anywhere else. . . . In short, yachting in America is now active in an area extending from the latitude of the English Channel to that of half way down the Red Sea and through the middle of the Sahara Desert. From west to east it covers an area comparable to that from Portugal to the Caspian Sea.' British yachtsmen in comparison have to find their cruising grounds around their own crowded coastline or that of neighbouring Europe, where the more desirable waters become even fuller.

Together with the moulded plastics revolution in boat construction the development of one particular design technique has brought new popularity to the smaller cruiser. This is the use of twin keels. While twin keel design is not new its extensive employment in such numerous classes of small cruiser has now introduced a new element into the world of small cruising yachts. Twin keels are able to confer a reasonably adequate degree of sailing ability on a yacht drawing perhaps only 60 per cent of the depth of water of a single keel design, while the keels enable the yacht to take the ground upright. These are two major advantages for cruisers intended for use in the inshore coastal and estuary areas which are the home waters for so many cruising families today. Such craft can do with less sophisticated and expensive shore facilities than the longer-legged, though admittedly faster, single keel yachts; while also, in the coastal congestion of today, being able to use shoal water areas debarred to deep draught boats.

Another development has helped to make the popular small cruiser of today; this is the use of caravan techniques in the layout and arrangements of the accommodation. Charles Dickens once wrote, startled and impressed, about his quarters in the early Cunarder *Britannia*, of how the stewardess produced things 'from the very entrails of the sofas, and from unexpected lockers, of such artful mechanism that it made one's head ache to see them opened one after another . . . to find every nook and corner and individual piece of furniture as something else beside what it pretended to be, and was a mere trap and deception and place of secret stowage . . .'

In the smaller cruising yacht of the past the limited space available was perhaps used too prodigally. Today, by means of high freeboard and cabin tops, a boat may have the same internal space as one of yesterday's for half the displacement tonnage, or total weight; and the space may be cunningly and economically used. We may compare a small cruiser in the older style with a typical representative of today. The Vertue type, of which several have crossed the Atlantic, is one of the most seaworthy types of small cruiser ever produced. On a length of 25ft 3in. (7·7m.) overall, a draught of 4ft 6in. (1·37m.), and a beam of 7ft 2in. (2·18m.) a Vertue is able to provide accommodation in moderate comfort for four. The Westerley 25 class of glass moulded cruiser has almost the same length and beam and also provides four berths; but with twin keels the draught is only 2ft 4in (0·71m.), while with a displacement tonnage of only 2 tons, compared with a Vertue's 4½ tons, the Westerly is adequately canvassed with 25 per cent less sail area. Here we see the anatomy of the older and the newer concepts of the small cruiser.

PAGES 44–45: Popular types of small modern stock cruisers of the Hood and Endeavour classes racing in Australian waters. Australian yachtsmen were originally prejudiced against moulded plastics hulls and stock designs; but have come to accept them.

OPPOSITE LEFT: For many years trawlers from Brixham in Devon were regarded as the most seaworthy and fastest fishing craft on the British coast. After 1918 the fleet dwindled in size; by the mid-1930s it was almost extinct. Yachtsmen favoured the craft as being suitable for conversion at reasonable expense into capable deep-water cruising yachts, and a number of the trawlers survived the fishing fleet in the role of yachts. By today's standards they made large cruisers, some of them more than 75ft (22·86m.) in length, 60ft (18·29m.) being a common size. The rig, in the latter years of the trawlers and retained on conversion into yachts, was the ketch, known among fishermen as the 'dandy' rig.

ABOVE: A few barges were converted into yachts by those who took a particular interest in this class of vessel and the specialized kind of seamanship associated with handling them – the skills of the bargemen who were known as 'sailormen' in London river and docks. With hulls which were almost oblong boxes though given some curved shape at the ends, and with a length perhaps exceeding 80ft (24·38m.) and a breadth of 20ft (6.1m.), a barge on conversion was able to provide spacious accommodation, and owners usually maintained them as floating homes. The spritsail is one of the oldest sails set by man, and *the* oldest fore-and-aft sail. The barge yacht shown here, *Seagull II*, is a relatively small craft, 43ft (13·11m.) in length, and was built in 1901. For working barges there was a celebrated annual race in the Thames estuary, and latterly a few well known barges were maintained for this purpose alone. The last of these races was sailed in 1963, just 100 years after the first.

LEFT: Sailing on the Norfolk Broads is a specialized and beguiling art. The penalties paid for mistakes in the narrow waters are comparatively trivial, if more public and embarrassing than those at sea; but the operations of sailing seamanship come in quick, sometimes hectic, succession between the banks of river or broad, and some special techniques are required when negotiating stretches where trees close in on either hand. Experienced deep-water seamen have found themselves in shame-making contretemps as the tortuous though harmless broads play them up.

CENTRE LEFT: The moorings in Sydney Harbour show several types of small modern cruiser, the one in the foreground being a moulded plastics stock boat; the smooth curves of the coach-roof will be noticed. Ahead of her is a type of chine hull, with an angle between topsides and bottom.

BELOW LEFT: The schooner rig carried by both the American yachts shown here was developed in its modern form in the U.S.A. during the last years of commercial sail. It was adopted readily in the yachting fleet, becoming in the U.S.A. the commonest rig in yachts of any size. In Britain there was a splendid period of racing in the largest schooners during the mid-nineteenth century, but later the racing superiority of the cutter rig was proved. Smaller schooner yachts were never common, as they were in the U.S.A., and today the yet further reduced size of yachts has made the rig generally unsuitable. The yacht in the foreground is of markedly traditional type in hull as well as rig, with clipper bow, short counter stern and gaff-rigged main and foresail, the latter only able to carry a topsail, which is not set in the illustration. Beyond her is a staysail schooner (i.e. the foresail is replaced by a staysail between the masts) and her mainsail is Bermudian.

RIGHT: A contrast in types: the spritsail barge carries a load of tradition and in rig has features dating back to the origins of sail. The Bermudian sloop has a rig of high efficiency for working to windward as developed by aerodynamics and wind tunnel research. The barge has her bowsprit steeved, or hinged upwards. Crudeness should not be imputed to the heavy rig of the barge. With a length of hull perhaps three times that of the yacht, the barge would carry a load many times the weight of the yacht while being handled by a smaller crew than required by the latter when racing.

ABOVE LEFT: The Chinese junk and its rig has been receiving attention from yachtsmen in recent years. Junk rigs, which vary in proportion on different parts of the coast of China, are all generically balanced lugs with numerous battens crossing the sails and a complex system of sheets leading from the aft ends of the battens. In this yacht certain junk characteristics of hull are also present.

The yachtsmen today is interested in the junk rig rather than its form of hull, and in yachts of modern hull design adaptations of the Chinese balanced lugsail are increasingly being set with the object of producing a rig more suited to the cruising yachtsman's purpose than the kind

50

of sail plan that has been evolved in the offshore racing fleet. The inspiration behind this trend has been Colonel H. G. Hasler's, who carried out experiments in the adaptation of the Chinese rig to modern requirements. By the use of terylene sails and ropes, plastic battens and possibly light alloy masts it has proved possible to transform into modern terms what has been described as the 'antique lash up of the China seas' rig', while retaining the cunning mechanical arrangements of the sails and rigging. Various non-Chinese deck arrangements enable the rig to be handled with less effort and skilful deckwork than required by the conventional yachts' rigs.

LEFT: The auxiliary gaff cutter *Oriette*, 34ft (10·36m.) in length overall, was built in 1924, and provides today a lively view of the traditional gaff rig. A topsail with a jackyard but no topsail yard is set above the mainsail; forward of the mast are a staysail, jib and jib topsail – five sails where the Bermudian sloop would set two. But *Oriette* is soon going to be reduced to three sails; for the crew, one out on the bowsprit and two at the foot of the mast, are engaged in setting a big blue balloon jib in place of the three headsails.

ABOVE: The gaff rig has not disappeared from the yachting scene, and *Penguin* and *Patsy* shown here are setting it, the latter to the right with a yardless jackyard topsail and a balloon jib on the bowsprit. Clearly, the number of ropes that have to be handled with this rig, compared with the Bermudian, together with the inconvenience of the bowsprit, and the fact that the rig is less close-winded than the Bermudian, are factors that do not add to its popularity; but today gaff-rigged yachts are able to bring variety and traditional grace to a sailing scene increasingly given over to displays of the isosceles triangle in sail shapes.

ABOVE: A gathering of modern cruising anchored at close quarters.

BELOW: While having the characteristics evolved by offshore racing, notably the tall narrow mainsail of small area and the large masthead genoa jib of appreciably more than the mainsail's area, such a yacht as is seen here under sail in Valletta Harbour, Malta, is also an admirable cruiser. She reveals the drawing together of the cruising and racing yacht which has been proceeding during the last quarter of a century. Today the smaller cruisers have drawn away from the cruiser-racer type, while the dedicated offshore racing yacht has now become as specialized as the inshore racing yachts of an earlier generation, though of greater seagoing ability.

RIGHT: The yacht approaching the camera, another schooner, is running down wind. The mainsail is lowered and she is carrying the rather unusual combination of twin spinnakers on respectively main and foremast.

Ocean Racing

The sport known generally as ocean racing now occupies a large sector of the yachting scene. Once the activity of a very few, it was exactly what its name implies. Since then the organization of ocean racing has spread its wings to cover much that is not in any sense oceanic in character.

It began amongst American yachtsmen and its most spectacular expression was the famous Bermuda race. Ocean racing spread to Britain, where it was not at first enthusiastically taken up, though the equally famous Fastnet race was instituted in 1925. In the early '30s there was some reason to expect that British and European ocean racing was going to die young. Then it picked up and by 1939 was firmly if modestly established. In the United Kingdom its organization was in the hands of the Royal Ocean Racing Club, which became and remains the only body in the world with a permanent headquarters and organization concerned with the sport. The corresponding body in the U.S.A, though less centralized and with no headquarters, is the Cruising Club of America.

Because the RORC evolved a rule of measurement for yachts and a more or less rational system of time allowance, enabling yachts of dissimilar size to race together, it found itself taking control of a kind of racing having nothing to do with the oceans. This included all forms of passage racing round the coast from port to port, generally known as offshore racing, and relatively short races – though they were long in comparison with regatta events – to foreign ports and in the North Sea and Channel; these might range between 150 miles and 300 miles in length.

During the three decades since the Second World War the Royal Ocean Racing Club, with its measurement system and time scale for handicapping, became the dominant authority in all yacht racing other than that of one-design and dayboat classes confined to regatta courses; this process was hurried on by the fact that the bigger kinds of class racing yacht had disappeared. Regatta racing for the bigger yachts, as well as offshore and ocean racing, became largely under the control of what in the 1930s had been a small club established for the sole purpose of organizing a few ocean races for a very few people with such strenuous taste. That is the position today; in 1975 the Royal Ocean Racing Club celebrated its jubilee.

The wheel going full circle, the ocean- and offshore-racing yachts have now returned for part of their time to regatta racing. The Admiral's cup, for example, now one of the major international yachting events, and introduced by the Royal Ocean Racing Club in 1957, includes in its programme two of the major offshore races, the Channel and the Fastnet, and two important round-the-buoys races forming part of the Cowes Week programme. It thus includes races of up to 605 miles in length, which may in light conditions occupy almost a week, to those occupying from breakfast to teatime in the Solent. The event is biennial; nations enter three yachts in their teams; a complex system of points based on the positions of yachts in the four races involved decides the issue. Yachts that may enter are limited in size between a fixed range of rating measurement, and the race results are corrected by time allowance based on each yacht's rating.

Time allowance is the essence of most yacht racing today other than in one-design classes. It has to be owned that no system of time allowance can be perfectly equitable, though experiments with various systems have now been proceeding for more than a century. When competition becomes keen enough, when large sums are laid out on yachts for particular events, the dedicated racing people will prefer not to have racing

influenced by the element of chance introduced by handicapping. Today a return has been made to level class racing via ocean racing – a curious evolution. In 1965 a trophy known as the One Ton Cup, originally raced for by yachts measuring one ton and later by those of the 6-Metre class (see page 28) was reintroduced, for yachts of fixed rating under the RORC rule, and therefore racing without time allowance. This was a return to the pre-war days of level racing between yachts of the larger sizes, but with a difference; that the yachts now race on courses both inshore and offshore in the course of the contest. There are now four cups offered for this form of racing, the Two-Ton, One-Ton, Three-Quarter-Ton and Half-Ton, for yachts of descending size.

1973–4; a Financial Times Clipper Race 1974–5, the first leg of which is from London to Sydney via the Cape of Good Hope, the second leg from Sydney to London via Cape Horn; there is the 1975–6 Whitbread Multi-Hull Race, covering a four legs course of 18,000 miles criss-crossing the north and south Atlantic.

All these races, inshore, offshore, oceanic and sometimes globe encircling, are the barely credible outcome of the first Fastnet and Bermuda races sailed by a handful of people with eccentric tastes.

PAGES 54–55: The parachute or balloon spinnaker, seen here set in a fresh following wind in *Sagittarius*, straining ahead of the hull and her other canvas, is the most stimulating sail set by modern yachts. Racing would be regarded as a tame sport today without the spinnaker. Of immense area compared with the rest of the canvas, like a circus tent and big enough to wrap round the boat, the fragile cloth and the great loads to which it is subjected – attached as it is to the boat at its three corners only – make the spinnaker the sailmaker's best friend. The fairy-like sail loads owners' pockets like interest on an overdraft, and gossamer though it may appear to be, ferocious battles on deck are fought to handle the sail when, as so often, control is lost.

LEFT: *Cervantes* is giving a demonstration of one kind of behaviour that a spinnaker may induce in a yacht. A complex trail of aerodynamic effects is able to set up fierce rolling which grows in amplitude in an awe-inspiring way. The roll of *Cervantes* has increased here until the outer end of the spinnaker pole is at moments touching the water, which can lead to a parting of gear and a subsequent exciting and possibly expensive operation getting the sail down. There is a liability for spinnakers to get foul aloft, when they have to be cut down in forlorn pieces.

ABOVE: The 24ft (7·32m.) waterline *Majical* is here experiencing the blowing out of her spinnaker. The man aloft has not, as might be supposed, been jerked up in an unguarded moment on the spinnaker halyard; he is being hoisted aloft on the forestay. The next operation will be to lower the pieces of the spinnaker. Large spinnakers have been known to blow out with something like an explosion, all remaining aloft afterwards being a circus hoop of the sails boundary.

In 1970 there occurred an event that would have sent the founding father of ocean racing, both British and American, reeling. A measurement rule for application worldwide came into force, known appropriately as the International Offshore Rule, directed by an International Offshore Rating Council. Thus today yachts racing in Fastnets or Bermudas, or in specially organised races half or wholly round the world, or in level racing events often over regatta courses, are measured by one common rule.

A feature of today's yacht racing is a small number of events, invariably richly sponsored and capable, in the hands of the right public relations organization, of obtaining wide publicity. Thus there was the Whitbread Round the World race in

LEFT: The start of the first Whitbread Round the World Race from Southsea Castle, at the entrance to Portsmouth, on the 8th September 1973. The event was a new conception organized by the Royal Naval Sailing Association and differing greatly in scale from conventional ocean racing, though similar in character. Essentially the contest comprised four ocean races, each in a grander manner than any formerly envisaged. There was a race from Portsmouth to Cape Town, 6,900 miles; from Capetown to Sydney, 6,500 miles; from Sydney to Rio de Janeiro, 8,370 miles; from Rio back to Portsmouth, 5,560 miles. The classic ocean races in the world today, the Bermuda, the Fastnet, the Sydney-Hobart range in length between 600 and 635 miles. The former longest conventional ocean race, the

Buenos Aires to Rio, is 1,200 miles. The figures emphasize how ambitious indeed was the conception of the Whitbread contest.

BELOW: News of the Whitbread contest raised a fleet of yachts, some specially built and strikingly larger than most ocean-racing yachts today. It was a deviation of the prevalent form in this age of midgets. The length of the races and the fact that a minimum crew per boat of six was stipulated encouraged this trend. One of the fleet was the sixth *Pen Duick* for Eric Tabarly, rigged less unconventionally than *Pen Duick III* as a Bermudian ketch, but an extreme type of craft, very light, with a narrow fin keel and ballast of uranium, which is nearly twice the weight of lead. But her spectacular design – even the

uranium – was not enough, and two
dismastings put her out of the contest.

RIGHT: One of the biggest new boats
entered for the race was *Great Britan II*,
78ft (23·77m.) in length overall, and like
Pen Duick VI a Bermudian ketch, though
of less extreme form and of bigger sail area.
The hull is built of glass reinforced plastic
foam sandwich. In charge of her was Chay
Blyth with a highly trained army crew
conditioned to accept standards of living
far from Lucullan while racing. Note the
characteristic Genoa headsail encouraged
by the offshore measurement rule under
which the yachts were raced. In November
1975, on the first leg of The Financial
Times Clipper Race, *Great Britain II* broke
the 106-year old record for non-stop
passage from London to Sydney.

BELOW: *Pen Duick III*, a long but light yacht
with shallow body and a bulb fin ballast
keel, 57ft (17·37m.) in length overall and
rigged as a very unconventional kind of
schooner, was brought out by Eric
Tabarly in 1967, and duly impressed and
surprised all who saw her when she came
to the line for her first race, the Royal
Ocean Racing Club's Morgan Cup,
starting and finishing at Portsmouth. She
won the race. The unusual sail between the
masts, which are of equal height, is carried
on a wishbone spar. Three such sails are
carried of different areas, the biggest
overlapping the sail on the second mast;
this, accepting the rig as a schooner, is
known as the mainsail, though of about
half the area only of the wishbone foresail.
This heavily canvassed yacht was usually
raced with a crew of nine.

FAR LEFT: *Kriter*, another large French entry in the Whitbread Round the World Race, is also ketch-rigged, but a yacht of less extreme type than *Pen Duick VI*, with more space on board for such home comforts as may be carried in yachts racing round the world. *Kriter* has a graceful clipper bow and shows an imaginative display of colour in hull and sails. The red sail between the masts is a large mizzen staysail set when running down wind.

LEFT: The classic ocean races sailed annually or biennially are tough contests engaged in by dedicated and skilful crews; races round the world, singlehanded or otherwise, are for a yet more exceptional breed. But every year nowadays, in north European, American and Mediterranean waters, there are held races of lengths around 180–250 miles which in fact are not strictly 'ocean' races, for they may not bring the yachts anywhere beyond the continental shelf, but entail day and night

racing as opposed to regatta racing by day. These are aptly described as 'offshore' races and appeal to those less intensely competitive and rugged than those who undertake the classics and the marathons. One of the most popular of these offshore races in Europe is the Royal Ocean Racing Club's Cowes-Dinard race, length 180 miles, which was first sailed in 1930 and has been held in every yachting season since then. Here the fleet are setting off, running eastward down the Solent.

BELOW: Over a long period now, indeed since the war, the boats at the smaller end of the offshore and ocean-racing fleet have steadily declined in size. In 1950 there was formed, chiefly at the instigation of Captain John Illingworth, then Commodore of the Royal Ocean Racing Club, the Junior Offshore Group, to cater for fast cruisers and offshore-racing craft of between 16ft (4·88m.) and 20ft (6·1m.) length on the waterline, which were below

the size recognized by the Royal Ocean Racing Club. In the U.S.A. a similar body, known as the Midget Ocean Racing Club, was formed a few years later, and the success of the two bodies indicates the revolution that has occurred in offshore racing attitudes. Since the '50s the class structure for racing has been several times adjusted, the senior club reducing its minimum size, and those below it being catered for by the Junior Offshore Group. Now classes are assessed by rating, not waterline length, and the four smallest classes belong to the junior group, though for certain races joining with the Royal Ocean Racing Club, when eight classes may be out racing. To the eyes of today the biggest of the Junior Offshore Group yachts appear quite sizeable craft, while the smallest – Class VIII – have proved themselves capable offshore-racing machines for the hardy. Here we see several classes of the Junior Offshore Group in a mixed fleet.

LEFT: The start of the Sydney-Hobart race in 1973. On this occasion 79 yachts from six countries competed – New Zealand, United States, Japan, Canada and Papua New Guinea as well as Australia. One of the two boats from the U.S.A. was the 12-Metre *American Eagle*, built for the defence of the America's Cup, but destined to be steered over many far flung finishing lines. Such an intrinsically fast boat may often be first across the line, as she was in the 1973 Sydney to Hobart race, but with the time allowance operating against her she may fail to win on corrected time. In the above race she also won the latter, and was the first yacht to achieve a first in both for 27 years.

BELOW LEFT: An American offshore-racing fleet in a crowded start.

BELOW: The Sydney to Hobart race was the third established of the triumvirate of major offshore races, and now like the Bermuda and Fastnet races it gathers entries from the waterfronts of the ocean-racing world. Over Christmas in the western hemisphere, fire-bound yachtsmen may hear radio reports of the race as it proceeds. Here the Australian yacht *Gingko* heads out of Sydney Harbour on the way to Hobart.

LEFT: Like other pictures in this chapter, the one of *Firebrand* here shows a lively situation racing under spinnaker. The wind is well forward, hence the spinnaker pole is sheeted almost over the stemhead, and the boat is heeling to a squall. The impression of speed under such conditions is liable to be greater than the speed itself; for with the hull at an extreme angle of heel and the rig operating under circumstances causing reduced efficiency, speed tends to drop in some proportion to the apparent fury of the occasion. This, and many other pictures shown here, serve to emphasize the strength and good engineering of modern yachts' rigs, with their metal masts and high tensile-strength rigging. They are far superior to flouncing sail spreads in yachts of an earlier day, whose canvas-clouded reputation for stalwart endurance may hide their weaknesses to our later day. One reason why small yachts are now able to maintain so fine a general level of sea-going ability is owing to the good engineering of their rigs.

BELOW LEFT AND RIGHT: Scenes during the contest for the Admiral's cup in 1975. The Belgian yacht *Dagon*, below left, is nearest the camera and all yachts are seen beating to windward in a moderate breeze; this was taken during the first inshore race of the contest. *Dagon*, of British design, also sailed for Belgium in the 1973 Admiral's cup series.

The illustration, right, shows very different conditions, the yachts running down wind in the lightest airs, with *Tenacious* (U.S.A.) nearest the camera and *Yeoman XX* ahead. Both were new boats in 1975. The latter was of extreme and successfully advanced design with a light, nearly flat-bottomed hull. In 1975 the Germans were holders of the cup, having won it for the first time in 1973, when sixteen nations were entered. Since the first races for the cup in 1957 there have been ten contests, held in alternate years. Nations entering have increased in number since 1957, when only Britain and the U.S.A. took part, to nineteen in 1975, when Britain won the trophy for the sixth time. Other nations to win it have been U.S.A. (1961 and 1969), Australia (1967) and Germany (1973).

America's
Cup Racing Today

From time to time during the years following World War 2 it was rumoured that America's Cup racing might be revived.

The last contest had been held in 1937 in the magnificent cutters of the J-Class, whose day was clearly over, not least because they required a professional crew of some 25 men. The critical question was what class should be adopted. The larger type of offshore yacht was considered, but the decision fell upon the 12-Metre class as being the largest pure racing yacht that might gain some support in the '50s and later. The 12-Metres had been the next largest international class to the J-boats in the pre-war days, though they were only about half the length and one-fifth of the displacement tonnage of the former. But

amongst the smaller yachts of the 1950s they seemed big indeed, expensive and lacking the versatility of the offshore racers.

A challenge was issued by the Royal Yacht Squadron in June 1957 for a contest to be sailed in the following year. The rules had to be adjusted to suit the smaller type of yacht and in the cause of greater fairness; conditions of America's Cup racing had leaned in the past towards favouring the defence. Though a 12-Metre with her racing rig modified was capable of sailing across the Atlantic, this condition for the challenge was withdrawn. It was also specified that the challengers might name another boat a week before the races should the initial challenger prove a disappointment. The contest was to be composed of the best out of seven races.

A syndicate of no less than a dozen members was formed to build the British challenger, an indication of how costly an America's Cup campaign had become despite the smaller yachts involved. The choice of the 12-Metre class gave an advantage to the U.S.A. which in the course of six contests between 1957 and 1974 has never been lost. In the U.S.A. was the 12-Metre *Vim* which, in the course of a season's racing in British waters in 1939, had proved herself outstandingly superior to any British Twelve. In Britain there was available as a yardstick boat only *Evaine*, which had been soundly beaten by *Vim* eighteen years earlier.

The defence was organized on the usual lavish scale, three new 12-Metres being built to meet the elderly lady of 1939, and the latter proved almost good enough to be selected for the

defence. Eventually the choice fell on one of the new boats, *Columbia*, by the firm of Sparkman & Stephens, who had also designed *Vim*. Meanwhile all was not well on the challenging side. The new boat *Sceptre* appeared at first to be little faster than *Evaine*. The challengers arrived in America nursing doubts.

These proved to be well founded. The contest itself proved to be a miserable mis-matching. The challenger lost four races in a row, one by more than eleven minutes. By the close of the contest it was clear that the U.S.A possessed four 12-Metre yachts each superior to the British challenger. In the U.K. earnest enquiries were set in motion to discover the reason why.

Since the first match for the America's Cup in 1870 all challengers had come from the U.K. except for two ineffectual contests when Canada had entered in 1876 and 1881. Only in the U.K. and U.S.A. was the large type of yacht demanded by America's Cup contests raced in any strength. By 1960 Australia had become a considerable yachting nation blessed by a climate ideal for the training of crews. Australia issued a challenge for 1962 through the Royal Sydney Yacht Squadron. The challengers chartered the redoubtable *Vim* against which to measure the abilities of the first Australian designed and built 12-Metre, the challenger *Gretel*. In the U.S.A. one new 12-Metre was built, the *Nefertiti*, but neither she nor *Colombia* were selected for the defence, the choice falling on *Weatherly*, which had been defeated by *Colombia* in 1958.

The contest between *Gretel* and *Weatherly* was a happy contrast to that of 1958. *Gretel* won the second race and lost the fourth by only 26 seconds. The race score then stood at 3:1, which might so easily have been 2:2. There were those who believed *Gretel* to be the better boat; more who thought she was better handled. But she lost the fifth and sixth races, and so became the eighteenth unsuccessful challenger.

Two years later another challenge came from the U.K. which showed too clearly that the reason for the 1958 defeat had not been learned. *Sovereign*, the new challenger, was a remarkable contrast in design to *Sceptre*, but out racing off Brenton Reef she proved to be no better. She had no competition worthy of the name during trials, whereas in the U.S.A was the finest fleet of 12-Metres in the world. *Constellation* was selected for the defence and she proceeded to beat *Sovereign* in four straight races, in the second of them by the staggering time of 20 minutes 24 seconds.

Now followed three more Australian challenges, in 1967, 1970 and 1974. *Constellation*, like *Vim* and *Colombia*, had been designed by the Maddison Avenue firm of Sparkman & Stephens – a firm with Olin Stephens at its head which might be regarded as the strongest weapon in the armoury of the Cup's defence. For the 1967 defence he produced one of the outstanding 12-Metres in the history of the class. This was *Intrepid*, destined to turn away the Australian challenges of 1967 and 1970 and then to come to the line again in the selection trials for the 1974 defender. In 1967 *Intrepid* defeated Australia's *Dame Pattie*.

In 1970 a new feature was introduced into America's Cup racing. It was a century since the first contest for the cup had been sailed in 1870; now for the first time it transpired that several challengers might appear simultaneously, and arrangements were made that in this case selection trials should be made between them. Thus, in 1970, a potential French challenger appeared, but she was beaten by Australia's *Gretel II*, which in turn was defeated by *Intrepid*.

Rules were altered for the 1974 contest, allowing the yachts to be built of aluminium alloy, one reason for this being a growing lack of shipwrights capable of the fine workmanship

required in building a 12-Metre yacht of timber. In the new material Australia produced *Southern Cross*; two new American boats were built, and the French entered again a potential challenger, the *France*, the same boat as in 1970. Also available for the defence in this year was, once again, *Intrepid*, by cup standards an old boat by this time; but her performance was that of proud confident youth. It seemed for a while that she might gain the unique distinction of defending the America's Cup three times in succession. But the new *Courageous* won through to selection by a very short head indeed. *France* was easily beaten by *Southern Cross*, which therefore became the challenger. She, though less easily, was beaten in her turn by *Courageous*, and she joined the unbroken long line of challengers that have failed.

PAGES 66–67: For the 1974 cup contest two new potential defenders were built, one of them, *Mariner*, of most unusual form and, as it transpired, of eccentric and unreliable performance. The other was *Courageous*, shown here. Both these new boats were of aluminium alloy, the latter by the designer of *Intrepid*.

ABOVE: The schooner *America* came over to the United Kingdom in 1851, the year of the Great Exhibition, and early showed herself to be a very fast yacht (see page 15). But the challenges for big

money prizes her owners had expected to receive did not materialize; her qualities may have caused some disquiet among the representatives of the premier yachting nation. She did, however, enter for a race round the Isle of Wight for a Royal Yacht Squadron Cup and was first home in the fleet of fifteen yachts.

The cup won by the *America* was presented for international competition by members of the original owning syndicate in 1857, when it was placed in the hands of the New York Yacht Club and became known as the America's Cup. No challenge was received until 1870, the first of the 22 which have taken place since then, all of them won by the defending American yacht. Some 150 years after the original *America* had won her race, a replica of the yacht, shown here, was out sailing in the Solent; it differs in small details from the original to make for greater comfort on board; for example, the original did not have a deckhouse.

OPPOSITE LEFT: *Evaine*, one of the best British pre-war 12-Metres, was available in 1958 when America's Cup racing was resumed. A new British yacht, *Sceptre*, was built as challenger, and *Evaine*, illustrated here, was refitted to sail against her. It was disturbing when *Sceptre* proved little better than *Evaine*, and indeed was often beaten by the latter; for it was known that, apart from any new Twelves, there was *Vim* in America, which in the last season before the war had proved much superior to *Evaine* when racing against her in English waters.

RIGHT: *American Eagle* was one of the two new American 12-Metres built for the defence of the America's Cup in 1964 against the second British post-war challenge. *American Eagle* and the other new potential defender *Constellation* proved to be in a class above former American Twelves, and it was evident that one of them would be selected as defender. At first it appeared likely that *American Eagle* would be chosen, but in the later trials *Constellation* worked out ahead and was selected. *American Eagle* had a varied career thereafter showing the fine qualities of 12-Metres when released from the specialization of cup racing. She crossed the Atlantic and competed in a number of Royal Ocean Racing Club events.

ABOVE: *Intrepid*, which won the contest against the second Australian challenger, *Dame Pattie*, in 1967 with almost insoucient ease, has proved to be one of the outstanding 12-Metres in the history of the class. She is an utterly ruthless racing machine, to the extent of having cabin linings of terylene cloth instead of wood panelling and furniture that is hardly usable, not only because it is made of spongy balsa wood but also being tucked away – and only just reaching conformity with the rules – into inaccessible corners.

RIGHT: *Sovereign*, Britain's challenger in 1964, out on early trials. After the debacle of the *Sceptre* challenge in 1958, special efforts were made to advance British 12-Metre design, and assistance was also received from the American model-testing tank in New Jersey, where the brilliant 12-Metres of the Cup defence had received the refinements to their lines. *Sovereign* was a remarkable contrast in design to *Sceptre*, though by the same architect, and not surprisingly her form of hull showed American influence. Another new British Twelve was built for the challenge, but the decision having been made late, there was time only to build a sister ship to *Sovereign*. Despite all efforts *Sovereign* proved in the Cup races to be as big a failure as *Sceptre*.

RIGHT INSET: *Gretel II* was the second victim of *Intrepid* when she was Australia's third challenger in 1970, and *Intrepid* defended the cup for the second time in succession. In many respects an advanced and adventurous design, *Gretel II*'s failure to achieve distinction in the contest was at least partially due to the disadvantage from which all challengers have suffered when competing with the U.S.A. – in American waters there is a distinguished fleet of 12-Metres ready to compete for the defence of the cup, each boat in the first class. The competition amongst them for selection as defender gives rise to the most intense 12-Metre racing in the world.

RIGHT: The American *Vim* might claim to be the most famous 12-Metre in the long history of the class. Racing in England during the 1939 season she won nineteen firsts, four seconds and two thirds in 27 starts against the best British yachts of the class sailing in their own home waters. She came near to selection as defender for the first post-war America's Cup contest in 1958 against three new boats, and remained for some years a yardstick for 12-Metre performance. She was chartered for four years in 1959 by the Australians when preparing for their first challenge, which took place in 1962.

LEFT: *Vim* is seen here racing against *Gretel I*. The latter was the first Australian challenger for the America's Cup; also the first yacht of this class to be designed or built in Australia. There were many who questioned whether, in these circumstances, Australia could produce a worthy America's Cup contender. But this was achieved triumphantly. *Gretel* proved a much superior challenger to the former British challenger *Sceptre* and the subsequent one, *Sovereign*. Certain imported materials were allowed for her construction, notably aluminium alloy extrusions for her mast and American sailcloth.

BELOW LEFT: In 1974 Australia produced *Southern Cross*, an unusual design of boat, for the challenge. It was for the first time permitted to construct 12-Metres in aluminium alloy, and *Southern Cross*, like all the other new boats, was in this material. She was tuned against *Gretel II*, Australia's challenger in the previous contest, and it became evident that she was a boat of high promise. There was also a potential French challenger, this again being *France*; but in the challenger selection trials, run by the Royal Thames Yacht Club off Newport, Rhode Island, *Southern Cross* swept to an easy victory. The stern view of this yacht shows the deck arrangement; the two steering wheels will be noticed.

Multi-hull and outrigged craft are alien to the Mediterranean and western traditions of sea-going. They belong to south-east Asia and the islands of Oceania. The multi-hull concept, however, has long been known in the west, and there are records of one such craft – a failure – being designed and built in Britain during the reign of Charles II. In yachting during the 1870s the brilliant American engineer and yacht architect, Nathaniel Herreshoff, experimented with catamarans of advanced mechanical design and under the right conditions achieved impressive enough speeds with them to disturb conventional opinion. The type was actively opposed and Herreshoff himself came to believe that for average speeds over any distance of seaway he could achieve better results with single hulled craft. The

experience we have today indicates that in this opinion he was wrong.

The rise of multi-hull craft to the position they now hold in the sailing world is a phenomenon of the last few decades only. The adoption of the primitive multi-hull and outrigger concepts and, in the manner of Herreshoff, applying sophisticated hydrodynamic and constructional techniques to them, has produced western versions of these types of marine craft which have proved to have a range of capabilities unexpected a few decades ago by all but a few enthusiasts.

Initially the object was to obtain higher maximum sailing speeds than are possible in single-hull craft. It has long been recognized that the upper limit of speed for the latter is low. It is due to the fact that to obtain higher speeds more power (i.e., sail area) is required; but more sail area demands more ballast to give it stability; as a result the power/weight ratio remains unaltered, weight of ballast chasing area of sail and the maximum speed possible remaining unaltered. By using outriggers or two hulls stability is divorced from weight, the required large sail area being held up by the spread of the hulls or outriggers not by weight and depth of ballast. The power/weight ratio is thus increased and with it the maximum potential speed.

By the early 1960s it had been most spectacularly demonstrated in the U.S.A. and Europe that for the highest speed over short courses the multi-hulls had undoubted superiority over the fastest types of single-hull planing craft as evolved in the racing-dinghy world. This had, indeed, been demonstrated by Herreshoff 80 years earlier; but now there were many more multi-hulls and also a general attitude of mind more sympathetic towards them. But might not Herreshoff's other belief also be true, that for average speeds over any appreciable distance of

more or less disturbed seaway the single-hull craft could hold its own with the multi-hull despite the latter's bursts of higher speed? The fact that the islands of the Pacific became inhabited as the outcome of prodigious ocean voyages in multi-hull craft suggested their sea-going ability; but there was (and remains) no general agreement as to how these voyages were conducted.

It was soon demonstrated, however, that the modern types of multi-hull craft were competent sea- and ocean-going vessels. In the Round Britain race of 1966 ten trimarans and catamarans and seven single-hull yachts took part, and the first six places in the race went to multi-hulls. That such a result could be achieved in the unpredictable and harsh coastal waters of the British Isles was astonishing to many. The victory for multi-hulls may have been less complete than it appeared; the boats in this class were outstandingly the best of their kind while the single-hull craft were of modest speed potential. Several of the multi-hulls were built specially for the race. The fact that the winner, the 42ft (12·8m.) trimaran *Toria*, was able to make an average speed of 6·9 knots gave her a performance beyond the capability of any single-hull boat of like length. Later Round Britain races and then the Singlehanded Transatlantic races could only add to the reputation – unwillingly recognized by the majority – of multi-hull craft for offshore and ocean sailing. It would have appeared astounding only a

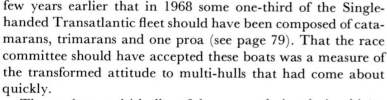

few years earlier that in 1968 some one-third of the Single-handed Transatlantic fleet should have been composed of catamarans, trimarans and one proa (see page 79). That the race committee should have accepted these boats was a measure of the transformed attitude to multi-hulls that had come about quickly.

The modern multi-hull craft bears an ethnic relationship to the Pacific boats, and luckily no more. The engineering of the structure, the aerodynamics of the rig have changed a rudimentary kind of craft into one of refinement and, to many, most unexpected capabilities. But apart from their sailing performance multi-hulls have proved to have an advantage of a more homely and widely acceptable kind; this applies particularly to catamarans, or craft with twin hulls. Using modern methods of design and construction it has proved possible, on a given length of boat, to provide more accommodation and greater sailing comfort for a family by using the catamaran configuration than is possible with a single hull, and to achieve this at a very much lower price. The latter fact is naturally of crucial significance. The cruising catamaran in which sailing performance may be of secondary importance is a new breed to the sailing waters of the world and one that has brought to the gentle art of unambitious cruising a particularly suitable kind of vehicle.

PAGES 74–75: Three types of craft compose the multi-hull fleets of today. We shall apply to them the names now generally in use without considering their etymology, about which there is often disagreement. First there is the trimaran, which has a central main hull given stability by an outrigger on either side. *Gulf Streamer* is a highly developed craft in this class. There are now great variety and scope for original design in the configuration of the form and the engineering of the various parts of multi-hulls. The original outrigger craft of Polynesia were composed of dugout main hulls, sometimes with additional sewn members, to which were lashed the cross struts, sometimes numerous, at whose outer ends were secured, again by lashing, the log outriggers. Details of such craft were first examined by Captain Cook and his successors who opened up the Pacific and studied the cultures of the islanders.

OPPOSITE FAR LEFT: The Australian *Miss Nylex* is a racing catamaran of exceptionally high performance. She sets a single solid balsa and fibreglass wing sail with flaps like those of aeroplane wings. She has been a winner in the Little America's cup series, the International Catamaran Challenge Trophy. In principle, a solid sail, especially one with flaps, is able to sail closer to the wind than the conventional soft sail, but no sail of this type has yet been produced which is suitable for ocean-going use.

LEFT: The trimaran *Pulau-Tiga* should be compared with *Gulf Streamer* (shown on the preceding pages). The difference in the cross members and configuration of the main hulls will be noticed. The narrowness of the latter will also be evident. This is an important element in the potential speed of such craft. Stability being given by the outriggers, wide beam is not necessary, as in most single-hull craft, to obtain the necessary degree of stiffness.

ABOVE: *Green Lady* is in marked contrast to *Gulf Streamer* and *Pulau-Tiga*. Here are three hulls braced together rather than a single hull with outriggers; it is a development carried beyond the concept of a single hull with a hollowed bottom, which was a form on which experiments were made in earlier years of high speed craft. The tunnels between the hulls result in a reduction of wetted surface and give a higher speed potential than is possible with a single hull; but there is a further advantage in this design, shared with the catamaran, that for a given length and displacement a great amount of space is available for accommodation spread over the hulls.

RIGHT: *Golden Cockerel* came in fifth place in the 1968 Transatlantic race, sailed by Bill Howell. Her catamaran configuration may be contrasted with the trimaran *Three Cheers*. She is American designed, of the Imi Loa class, normally sloop-rigged for racing, but for ocean work *Golden Cockerel* was given a staysail ketch rig. In comparison with *Three Cheers* her accommodation is relatively generous, and though such a successful type of racing craft, *Golden Cockerel*, 43ft (13·11m.) in length overall, is of the type of the high performance cruising catamaran.

FAR RIGHT ABOVE: In the Transatlantic Singlehanded race of 1968 there was entered the proa *Cheers*, sailed by Tom Follett. She had two hulls 40ft (12·19m.) in length connected by cross beams at a distance apart of some 16ft (4·88m.). The crew and most of the weight was in one of the hulls, the boat being designed on the principle that the heavier, man-occupied hull should always be on the same side as the wind. The rig had thus to be arranged so that the boat might sail first with one end leading, then the other, a startling concept to western ideas of sailing seamanship. After some adjustments, following a capsize in the Caribbean, to give improved stability, *Cheers* was accepted by the race committee, which initially had not been enthusiastic about the craft: 'We are still of the opinion that to race along at 25 knots in between periodically capsizing is not a proper way to cross the Atlantic', was their observation at one stage. *Cheers* not only completed the course successfully, but came in third place, led over the line by two single-hull craft.

FAR RIGHT CENTRE: The successor to *Cheers* was *Three Cheers*, a 46ft (14·02m.) trimaran and therefore equipped with a more conventional rig. In the 1968 Transatlantic Singlehanded race thirteen out of 35 entries were multi-hulls; in 1972 there were only seven out of 55 entries. But those seven gained the first, third, fifth and sixth places. Such results could only transform former attitudes to the ocean-going capabilities of multi-hull craft.

FAR RIGHT BELOW: Racing catamarans of the International Yacht Racing Union A and B classes sailing in Sydney harbour. They are on a course with the wind free under conditions that would give them their highest speeds should a gust spring up. The A class was devised to produce boats for singlehanded racing, the first appeared in Britain in 1962. Note the fully battened sails of both boats.

LEFT: *Unicorn* is shown here sailing under ideal conditions for high speed, with the actual – as opposed to the apparent – wind slightly abaft the beam. To obtain the best speed out of the catamaran configuration of hulls the craft is sailed with the weather hull lifted out of the water, as it appears here. It will be noticed that the hull has a centreboard, and that a una rig is carried, without any headsail or jib.

BELOW LEFT: Eric Tabarly, having won the Singlehanded Transatlantic race in 1964 with *Pen Duick II*, an unexceptional single-hull ketch, was reaching the conclusion by the end of the '60s that a multi-hull craft was the obvious choice for winning the race, and of these he preferred a trimaran. He also believed that light aluminium alloy was the ideal material for constructing fast sea-going yachts. The outcome of his ideas was the 66ft (20·12m.) trimaran *Pen Duick IV*, shown here, and a monstrous boat she seemed to many when she came to the line for the Singlehanded Transatlantic race of 1968. From certain angles when out of the water she had a spidery grace and a strength which this appearance belied, thanks to her welded alloy construction. She was at that time recently completed and unprepared for the race; her rigging was in particularly poor shape. She did not complete the course. But in the 1972 Transatlantic, after Tabarly had sold her to his countryman Alain Colas, she was sailed to victory, beating the freak single-hull craft *Vendredi XIII* (see page 90) by sixteen hours. As the present author wrote at the time of the race: 'Twelve years ago the winner of this year's race would have been regarded as an instrument of suicide and the second boat as fantastic'.

RIGHT: The catamaran has two hulls of equal size braced together side by side. This, and not the trimaran, is believed to have been the principal ocean-going craft of the Pacific in times before the arrival of Europeans. Some of these craft reached great size; a few of those which survived to be examined by the European explorers were as much as 100ft (30·48m.) overall. *Hellcat*, shown here, is a small racing catamaran and one of a series of boats with the same name in which the design of catamarans was advanced in the course of the '60s. Their designer was R. Macalpine-Downie, one of the pioneers in this branch of design for sail.

The Boats
of the
Lone Sailors

A small group of men have elected from time to time to sail the oceans on their own since Captain Joshua Slocam led the way round the world singlehanded during 1895–98. There became more of such people than hitherto during the 1950s; but it was not until the institution of the Singlehanded Transatlantic race in 1960 that this esoteric activity became an organized one.

The idea of the race was Lieutenant-Colonel H. G. Hasler's. Experienced in conventional ocean racing, he was not satisfied with the rule-controlled, large-crewed typical offshore-racing yacht, which he considered had become an unsuitable type to influence in the right direction the true ocean-cruising yacht. The race was sponsored by the London Sunday newspaper, the 'Observer' and handled by the Royal Western Yacht Club of England, whose name was written deeply on the history of yachting through their organization of the first Fastnet race in 1925. There were but five starters for that first Singlehanded Transatlantic Race in 1960, including Hasler himself and Francis Chichester (later Sir) but an important principle had been established. The boats eligible for the race might be of any size or type – the limitation was the purely physical one that they had to be handled by one man – though the Race Committee of the Royal Western had the exacting power of disqualifying any clearly unseaworthy craft. The race was won by the largest boat entered, Chichester's *Gipsy Moth III*, 40ft (12·19m.) in length overall. Hasler was second in his little junk-rigged Folkboat *Jester*, in all but the unusual rig a good example of the smallest cruising yacht of the day.

Four men in four boats led the way to the remarkable series of Singlehanded Transatlantic races which have taken place every fourth year since 1960. The entries have increased progressively from the four of the first race to 55 boats in 1972. The types and sizes of boats that have become involved would have appeared disturbing to conventional maritime attitudes as late as 1960. In the 1968 race thirteen of the 35 entries were multi-hull craft. In 1972 the race was won by the 67ft (20·42m.) long aluminium alloy trimaran ketch *Pen Duick III* which had not a little to alarm the Race Committee when Eric Tabarly had brought her to the line in 1968. She was ill prepared for this race, but Tabarly's countryman Alain Colas sailed her to victory in the next. In the same year the second boat across the line was in some quarters regarded as a monster – a single-hull singlehander no less than 67ft (20·42m.) long, rigged with three masts carrying under full sail a masthead staysail on each, and perversely named *Vendredi 13*. Hardly less shocking to conventional tastes was the third boat to finish, the proa *Cheers*. The freedom of design allowed under the rules of the Singlehanded Transatlantic was leading to results not, some felt, perfectly aligned with desirable yachting developments.

During 1966–7 Francis Chichester made his singlehanded voyage round the world with one stop in Sydney. Already a celebrated professional navigator with his yachts named after the aircraft with which he had made pioneering long-distance flights, his *Gipsy Moth IV* was designed for him to make faster time, if possible, to Australia than the clipper ships that had once traded on the route. The voyage was attended by the publicity raised through modern sponsorship and communications media, which brought the adventure to millions of homes. The speeds achieved by Chichester on his voyage out and home were a tribute to modern yacht design, but above all to the indomitable spirit of a man in late middle age.

It was a similar spirit in a man just a little younger that sent Alec Rose on a similar voyage round the world in the following year. Without sailing as slowly as Slocam and those who fol-

lowed immediately in his wake – Harry Pidgeon in his *Islander*, Alain Gerbault in *Firecrest* – Alec Rose aimed at no records, but he had no intention of spending too long on the voyage to Australia and back.

The idea that the world might be circumnavigated under sail not only singlehanded but also non-stop may have occurred to some people prior to 1968; whether it was a sensible idea, whether indeed the modern sailing yacht was advanced enough technologically to achieve this, was at the time doubted by people competent to judge. When Robin Knox-Johnston achieved the feat, and in a yacht of no exceptional capability, both questions were presumably in some way answered. When a few years later Chay Blyth undertook to sail round the world singlehanded, non-stop and in the contrary direction (from east to west) to all the dictates of traditional seamanship and world meteorology, the same questions might have been asked

again; but by this time the spirits of the lone seamen were recognized as being unconquerable. The 'Impossible Voyage' was accomplished.

The worlds of their own of the lone sailors cannot be entered by those on the outside. We know their craft, perhaps intimately. We can never really know *them* – those who are lone sailors at heart out to conquer, with no company to support them, not only the sea but the Everests of the mind faced by the lone navigator.

PAGES 82–83: The little *Suhaili*, a spot on the ocean below. Like Sir Alec Rose's *Lively Lady*, *Suhaili* was built in India entirely of teak, and the Bombay shipwrights who worked on her used the traditional boatbuilding methods and tools that had been the common practice when their forefathers built Royal Navy ships

in the nineteenth century. Owing to her rig, with the mizzen boom overhanding the stern, an unusual arrangement of self-steering gear was necessary, and this broke down in the course of the voyage. But *Suhaili* (see also page 91) proved to be beautifully balanced, enabling her lone hand to continue the voyage.

ABOVE: When the first of the Singlehanded Transatlantic Races was organized in 1960 one of the five boats to compete was *Gipsy Moth III* owned and sailed by Francis Chichester (not yet knighted). He had yet to make his great reputation in sail. *Gipsy Moth III*, the largest of the boats competing, won the race. With a length overall of 40ft (12·19m.), she was typical of the medium-sized offshore-racing yacht of the time, a moderate type of cruiser-racer, designed by Robert Clark, well known for this type of boat, who in the years following created several other yachts for lone sailors, including Chay Blyth's *British Steel* (see page 93) and *Sir Thomas Lipton* (see page 90) winner of the Singlehanded Transatlantic Race in 1968.

BELOW: Also in the first Singlehanded Transatlantic Race was the junk-rigged *Jester*. This tiny yacht, whose hull is that of the standard Scandinavian Folkboat with an overall length of 25ft (7·62m.), has been sailed across the Atlantic singlehanded some half a dozen times. The hull is conventional enough; not so the rig, which is the modern version of the Chinese junk rig developed by Colonel H. G. Hasler, her owner in 1960, when he was responsible for initiating the Singlehanded Transatlantic Race. The rig, and the layout of the deck, enabling the boat to be handled from a sheltered position amidships, was the outcome of long and careful development by Hasler, his

inspiration being a belief that the conventional yachtsman's rig as used in offshore-racing yachts was not the most suitable that could be devised for those who wish to sail alone or with only a small crew on long voyages.

BELOW RIGHT: When Commander W. King had a boat designed for a singlehanded non-stop voyage round the world he selected for it the Hasler-conceived junk type of rig. The boat, *Galway Blazer*, like *Jester*, had a most unusual deck layout designed to suit the lone sailor under the worst conditions, and the junk sails were set on two masts in a schooner rig. The masts were unsupported by standing

rigging in the Chinese manner. Twice, in trying to complete the circumnavigation, *Galway Blazer* struck misfortune. She was rolled over and had the masts broken when about 1000 miles south-west of Cape Town; and on a second attempt the hull was holed by a shark.

RIGHT: By 1971 Sir Francis Chichester had conceived a fresh sailing ambition. Put in its simplest terms, this was to sail single-handed and non-stop for a distance of 4,000 miles at an average speed of 200 miles per day. The first necessity was to select a suitable course, giving the required distance in an area where strong fair winds would prevail – the essential requirement

if the speed target was to be attained. The second was to find a suitable yacht with a rig capable of giving high down-wind speeds. The hull of *Gipsy Moth V* is similar to that of *Sir Thomas Lipton* (see page 90) but the usual staysail ketch rig was devised to suit the yacht's exceptional purpose. The target speed of 200 miles per day was a high ambition, not quite achieved; but over a course between Bissau in Portuguese Guinea to Greytown some 120 miles north of Panama, an average speed of 179·1 miles a day was maintained.

For his circumnavigation of the world
in 1966–7 Francis Chichester had a
yacht – *Gipsy Moth IV* – designed for his
purpose, which was to make the passage to
Australia and back in better than the
average time taken for the voyage out and
return by the clippers; this was estimated
at 100 days out and 110 days home. His
requirement therefore was as fast a yacht
as possible under the limitation of singlehanded sailing. Chichester failed in his race
against the clippers, but his voyage out to
Sydney and back to Plymouth was watched
with mounting interest by millions on
radio, television and in the newspapers,
and he returned to a knighthood.

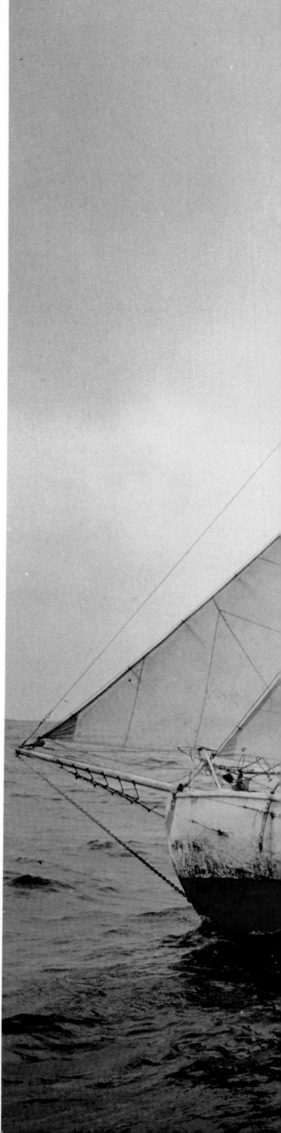

TOP: For the third Singlehanded Transatlantic Race Geoffrey Williams had designed and built specially for the purpose *Sir Thomas Lipton*, a remarkably sleek and handsome Bermudian yawl with a slim hull no less than 57ft (15·85m.) in length overall, which was large indeed for a singlehander. But the pretty blue-masted yacht won the race against 34 others.

ABOVE: The fourth Singlehanded Transatlantic Race in 1972 produced several unusual boats among the 55 competitors, and none more startling to conventional eyes than the perversely named *Vendredi 13*. Someone suggested that she put the art of design back 600 years. No less than 128ft (39·01m.) in length, 80 per cent longer than the next largest yacht in the race, she reached towards the ultimate in size possible for a craft capable

of being handled by one man. To drive the hull a rig which can be given no name was devised. It was composed of three staysails set on three masts; but the sail area was small in proportion to the size of boat to bring it within the power of control of a lone hand, and the slowness of the boat in light winds cost her the race. She came in second to the trimaran *Pen Duick IV*.

RIGHT: In 1968 *The Sunday Times* (London) offered an award to the first person to sail singlehanded and also non-stop round the world. This was achieved by the small ketch *Suhaili*, 32ft (9·75m.) in length, handled by Robin Knox-Johnston. Essentially a simple boat with no exceptional characteristics or inherent speed potential, she proved capable of being the instrument of one of the greatest epics in singlehanded seamanship.

LEFT: During 1967–8 Sir Alec Rose completed his circumnavigation which gained no less public attention than Sir Francis Chichester's during the previous year. His yacht was *Lively Lady*, a conventional, robust type of cruising yacht of the type favoured in the 1930s, very stoutly built in India of teak throughout. She had not the speed of *Gipsy Moth IV*, but Rose was not aiming at records. To sail to Australia and back singlehanded, rounding Cape Horn in the process, and to visit relations in Australia were objects enough. On the return voyage rigging trouble forced him into Bluff, New Zealand. The yacht's rig is unusual; she carries two masts, yawl fashion, but the purpose of the mizzen is solely to set a mizzen staysail instead of the mainsail in light winds. This bow view of *Lively Lady*, shown here being launched in a cradle on the slipway, reveals her full hull form. It is a type of yacht providing a generous amount of space below deck. With a length of only 36ft (10·97m.) overall and by no means broad in proportion, *Lively Lady* is a heavy and commodious yacht compared with the average small cruiser of today, which may be two-thirds of her length and barely a third of her weight.

RIGHT: Robin Knox-Johnston sailed round the world non-stop in the conventional direction, going eastward round the two Capes in the sailing ship tradition, gaining advantage of the westerly winds and easterly current of the Roaring Forties. There seemed few peaks left for the lone sailor to conquer. Chay Blyth found one; to sail non-stop round the world in a westerly direction. This entailed the ultimate sailing rigour of butting head-on into the worst seas in the world where the Southern Ocean encircles the globe and the current known as the West Wind Drift is in opposition. Such a voyage may have been a perverse ambition, but it was a self-imposed test of human endurance of which Blyth had made a practical study. Only an exceptional yacht could withstand the rigours of such a voyage, and *British Steel*, designed and built for the purpose, was certainly the strongest, most expensive and most carefully devised singlehander yet to have appeared. A large craft, 5ft (1·52m.) longer than *Gipsy Moth IV*, very much heavier and with a sturdy Bermudian ketch rig, *British Steel*, like the man who handled her, proved equal to an exceptional trial.

Sailing alone for long periods imposes tests physical and mental which only a few can withstand, as well as dangers that many have no wish to face voluntarily. Donald Crowhurst was sailing round the world in the catamaran *Teignmouth Electron* in pursuit of the same award as Robin Knox-Johnston, but his was the tragic way. Leaving the record of a log showing progressive stages of mental deterioration, he went overboard, and the catamaran was found drifting off the south coast of England.

Metrication Note

Imperial units of measurement, other than recognized boat classes (e.g. International 14 foot) are followed by their metric equivalents, given in parentheses. An exception has been made in the case of nautical miles and knots – recognized shipping units – and tons. Imperial tons (and the closely allied tons Thames measurement) have not been converted as they so nearly equate to the metric tonne.

Index

Acknowledgments

The publishers would like to thank the following organizations and individuals for their kind permission to reproduce the photographs in this book:

Australian News and Information Bureau: 62–63 above, 63 below right; Douglass Baglin: 42–43, 72 above, 73, 79 below right; Diana Beeston: 48 below, 52 above left, 52–53; Beken of Cowes: 1, 11, 12 above, 18–19, 21 below, 22 above, 23, 26–27, 29, 30, 31 above, 34–35, 47, 50 above, 54–55, 57 above right, 58 below, 59 above right, 60–61, 68, 69, 74–75, 76–77, 77 above right, 78–79, 79 above and centre right, 80, 86–87, 90; Alastair Black: 2–3, 38 below, 39, 40, 64 below, 65; J. Allan Cash: 24 above, 37, 50–51, 56–57, 59 below, 64 above, 70 above right, 88–89; Cassell and Co. Ltd: 90–91 (photograph originally reproduced in Robin Knox-Johnston's "A World of My Own"); Francis Chichester Ltd: 84–85; Crown Copyright, Science Museum, London: 8, 10, 12 below; Daily Telegraph Colour Library: 19 above right, 32–33 below; Ron Dorman: 28 above, 44–45, 48 centre; Michael Holford: 13, 14–15 above; The Illustrated London News: 58 above left; Claire and Bill Leimbach: 4–5, 41 above right, 46, 49; National Maritime Museum: 6–7, 9, 14 below, 15; Picture-point Ltd: 20, 21 above, 22 below right, 24 below, 25, 28 below, 32 above, 36, 41 left, 50 below, 52 below left, 70–71, 81; Ian Proctor: 31 below, 38 above, 48 above; Sir Alec Rose: 92 (photograph originally reproduced in Sir Alec Rose's "My Lively Lady", Nautical Publishing Co. Ltd.); Stanley Rosenfeld: 42 above left, 62–63 below, 66–67, 70 above left and below right, 72 below; Sea Spray Magazine, Sydney, Australia: 42 centre left, 76 left; Roger Smith Photography, Cowes: 33 above; Syndication International: 82–83, 90–91, 93, 94; Transworld Feature Syndicate Inc: 16–17, endpapers; Yachting World: 33 below right.